"In 5 Puritan Women, Jenny-Lyn de Kl[...] who have gone before us. As you get to [...] of this book, you will feel as though you have met five new friends. Through their words and stories, they will instruct, strengthen, and encourage you in your faith. So grab a warm drink, sit down with your new friends, and let them spur you on to love God and live a faithful, beautiful life."

Courtney Doctor, Coordinator of Women's Initiatives, The Gospel Coalition; Bible teacher; author, *From Garden to Glory* and *In View of God's Mercies*

"At some point, someone somewhere must have convinced me to believe the Puritans were boring. But as it turns out, that person was dead wrong. In *5 Puritan Women*, Jenny-Lyn de Klerk shakes the dust off the stories of five women we never should have overlooked. Their remarkable strength, distinct personalities, and substantial faith offer women today an unexpected and delightful inheritance that can impact the way we express and enjoy our faith today."

Caroline Saunders, author, *The Story of Water; The Story of Home;* and *Good News*

"We are all prone to stereotypes and misunderstanding, but part of loving our neighbors—even dead ones!—is seeking to understand them on their own terms so that we can better appreciate and learn from them. Jenny-Lyn de Klerk has written a book about five Puritan women who faced real challenges in a real world with their real God. What she also helps us (both men and women) learn from these godly mentors is significant. I'm only sad it has taken us this long to hear from these too-often-forgotten saints."

Kelly M. Kapic, Professor of Theological Studies, Covenant College; author, *You're Only Human*

"Often neglected, usually misunderstood, and grossly maligned, the Puritan women of the past are far overdue for a revival. Agnes Beaumont, Lucy Hutchinson, Mary Rich, Anne Bradstreet, and Lady Brilliana Harley should be household names. For not only did they contribute robust theological insights of their own, but they mastered the Christian life by exemplifying with profound maturity the love of Christ, a love so absent from our relationships with one another today. Who better to bring about this revival than a talented, even magical writer who embodies the spirit and theology of these Puritan women herself? Look no further than Jenny-Lyn de Klerk. She has not only become a kindred spirit with these Puritan women, but she has given them a voice. May the resiliency of their religion and the fervor of their faith infuse the church today until it becomes the spiritual family envisioned by our Lord."

Matthew Barrett, Associate Professor of Christian Theology, Midwestern Baptist Theological Seminary; author, *Owen on the Christian Life*

"Discover the extraordinary lives and deeply inspiring and insightful writings of the five women in Jenny-Lyn de Klerk's illuminating new book. Each of these Puritan women deserve to be better known by Christian readers. Their words are infused with the evidences of intimate, daily experience of God's living word, and their spiritual wisdom is on par with any well-known saint in Christian history, with enduring relevance. The lives of Agnes Beaumont, Lady Brilliana Harley, Mary Rich, Anne Bradstreet, and Lucy Hutchinson traced every conceivable extreme of joy and suffering that the seventeenth century could present, and yet they demonstrated what it means to persevere in love, with mercy, and in full assurance of salvation. This is an accessible, much-needed, and soul-enriching book that you will not regret having read."

Johanna Harris, Senior Lecturer in English, University of Exeter

5 Puritan Women

5 Puritan Women

Portraits of Faith and Love

Jenny-Lyn de Klerk

WHEATON, ILLINOIS

for my husband,
who "ha[s] wisdom and virtue enough to
be trusted with [my] counsels"

Contents

Foreword

IMAGINE BEING THE WOMAN who hitched a ride to church one day with John Bunyan (yes, *that* John Bunyan), then was wrongly suspected of having an affair with the renowned Baptist preacher, and later falsely accused of murdering your own father—only to be all but written out of the pages of history.

That is essentially what happened to Agnes Beaumont, a seventeenth-century Puritan, whose fascinating but forgotten life has much to offer us today, from glimpses into an intriguing period of history, to a better understanding of longstanding denominational divisions, to personal encouragement toward Christian faithfulness amid hard trials and temptations.

Of course, history is replete with forgotten stories of faithful saints. The great cloud of witnesses is voluminous. This is why it is always a gift to the present (as well as to the future) for neglected lives from the church of ages past to be brought forward again for our edification and instruction. It is an even more precious gift when such stories are presented by a skillful researcher and talented writer whose offering is not only an act of scholarship, but also an act of faith and worship. Such is the gift Jenny-Lyn de Klerk provides here.

While every era within church history is peopled by many lives worth remembering, these stories of devout Puritan women offer particular insights that are timely for the church today.

First, the lives and beliefs of Puritans (especially Puritan women) tend often to be cloaked in misunderstandings, distortions, and expectations that obscure the power of their examples. History is where we turn to get past the stereotypes, as clearly evidenced by the histories of the women profiled here. Beneath the veneer of easy assumptions, these women display a conservative theology that cultivates richness rather than narrowness, rigor rather than weakness, and abundance rather than austerity. Even so, their stories are complex. Their lives—like the lives of many of us—are marked at times by pride, disobedience, insecurity, confusion, loss, and despair. Yet, they also exhibit—as we aspire to as well—sanctification, strength, perseverance, buoyance, and faithfulness. These women have earned their rightful places in the church among other faithful theologians, philanthropists, poets, daughters, wives, sisters, and parents simply through their faithfulness and in using their gifts for the church.

Their lives, being of particular times, places, and circumstances, nevertheless offer illuminations for our own times and applications for all believers. Though our culture seems very different from that of the Puritans, both ours and that of the seventeenth century were significantly shaped by new forms of technology. We, as they were, have been overwhelmed by new floods of information (and disinformation), debates, controversies, and divisions—all of which are multiplied and amplified by new technologies (in their case, print; in ours, digital media). Furthermore, just as it was during the Puritan age, the church of our day is heated by controversies and divided by theological debates. The believers of ages past underwent refining fires like those many of us today sense the church is undergoing. The stories of these exemplary Christian women carry all this forward into our own time for our benefit.

"What has been is what will be, and what has been done is what will be done, and there is nothing new under the sun," the writer of Ecclesiastes tells us (Eccles. 1:9 ESV). Some, if not all, of the lives and stories of the women in these pages will be new to many readers. Yet, to a one, their testimonies, even in their uniqueness and interesting detail, remind us that God's truths and faithfulness never change.

KAREN SWALLOW PRIOR
Southeastern Baptist Theological Seminary

Preface

Discovering Kindred Spirits in Church History

HAVE YOU EVER HAD an emotional or intellectual epiphany so significant that it changed your way of being for years to come? When I first pulled a book by a Puritan woman off some library stacks, I was not ready for what I would find. Five years earlier I had experienced a theological awakening of sorts when I began to read John Owen and was introduced to a better way of understanding Scripture as taught by the Puritans—those seventeenth-century English believers who wanted to keep reforming the church and taught a heartfelt kind of holy living. I thought I had now moved on from this early stage, marked by the repeated thrills and inability to put a book down that comes with any new start. But now I had found something that I did not know was missing from my self-understanding as a Christian, a woman, and a writer—the wisdom of the female Puritans. The day I read my first poems and letters by Puritan women, I began another season of discovery, excitement, and insight—a spiritual awakening—as I learned from historical figures that I could relate to even more than others I had read. Questions I didn't realize I had tucked away in the bottom of my soul for safekeeping began to rise to the surface and find expression in the words of these women, and I found my heart giving the same answers as theirs. We shared a common Christian experience.

To my shame, these women were there the whole time, and I didn't even know it! But what I have found since then—after adding their stories to my own writings and lectures on the Puritans—is that no one else had known them either, and they had the same effect on other students (young and old) that they had on me, even in the small amount of time they spent getting to know them. Sadly, I could not find many books to suggest for further reading, especially to church folk interested in spiritual growth. Most of the academic resources I had studied would be of little use to this group at best and frustrating at worst, not only because they are too technical but also (in some cases) because they attempt to squeeze real Christian women who lived hundreds of years ago into the contrived paradigm of a practically atheistic, modern-day woman. The actual writings of the women themselves are also not easily accessible, as many are only available in expensive critical volumes or poorly formatted online versions that have no commentary to help readers make meaning out of their dulled font.

Thus, I decided to write something myself—this book—for all you lovely church folk who want to meet these women or are looking for inspiration in your spiritual journey, especially when it comes to your relationships with God and family. There are so many gems for Christians to find in reading women from church history, as aspects of their stories are not only timeless but also universal and thus relevant for believers of all sorts. In fact, the women in this book represent the Anglican, Presbyterian, and Baptist traditions. And as Lucy Hutchinson herself said, "I desire to own as brothers and sisters" all believers, regardless of their denomination.[1] So whoever you are, I'm certain you'll not only discover interesting artifacts in the pages to come but also kindred spirits you can relate to on a personal basis.

As was the case with these female Puritan authors, many friends have helped me reach the place of writing this book. First, a special thanks is due to Karen Swallow Prior for generously agreeing to write the foreword, one that does justice to the beauty and complexity of its subjects. I am also grateful for such brilliant scholars as Johanna Harris, Crawford Gribben, Raymond Anselment, and David Norbrook, whose work on Puritan women has opened my mind to new ideas and whose personal encouragements have given me confidence in my own work. Last, I would like to thank my many colleagues and mentors at Ambrose University (Calgary, AB), Regent College (Vancouver, BC), and Midwestern Baptist Theological Seminary (Kansas City, MO), my friends at various churches in the greater Vancouver area, and, most importantly, my family, all for helping me become the person I am now as I write this book. Your years of cherishing, teaching, and supporting have not been lost on me.

Introduction

Testimonies of Love

Advocacy, Barefaced and Unashamed

Before you read any further, I have a confession to make. If I may use the words of J. I. Packer, a long-time defender and promoter of the Puritans, "The present [book] is, I confess, advocacy, barefaced and unashamed. I am seeking to make good the claim that the Puritans can teach us lessons that we badly need to learn."[1] In other words, I wrote this book as someone who believes what the Puritans believed and commend them to us today as mentors worthy of our trust and emulation. But why is this a confession, or something that needs to be admitted? The reason Packer spoke of his teaching on the Puritans in this way was because he knew, maybe better than most, that many assume the worst of the Puritans. This group has been unfairly maligned since their own time and not much has changed, at least when it comes to popular thought.

Sadly, this is only more true for Puritan women. Of course, the writings and work of women in general have been largely neglected until the past few decades. But this is not the only reason Puritan women have been pushed aside—it is also because they do not always say what modern historians want them to say. I wish it were not true, but the proclamation to listen to women, believe women, and appreciate women as unique individuals is sometimes only applied to those who can fit within our current culture's belief system without too much force. In fact, those who do not fit into this system are, at times, seen as a potential danger to the cause of reviving women's writings. Now, this is not always the case; there are some excellent academic resources on Puritan women that do not feel the need to toss them out or mold their lives into a shape that looks more like ours. But my generalization remains true. I cannot count how many times I have read articles that literally argue these women said the exact opposite of what they actually said or how many times I've mentioned doing research on Puritan women and been met with looks of astonishment, confusion, and even disgust: "Why would such a young, smart girl like yourself want to waste her time with the submissive, uptight, quintessentially *puritanical* wives of those patriarchalists?" "Do you often come across stories of neglect, sexism, and abuse?" "I'm sure they could not even file for divorce!"

Sparking a Reading Revival

You may think I am joking, but this is not far from real conversations I have had and gets to the heart of what I want to say in this introduction: that there is a need to revive the writings of Puritan women for Christians today by reading them on their own terms, which is what this book seeks to do. Contrary to how many imagine these women, they were not forbidden from leaving the house, prevented from using their human agency, or even incapable of getting divorced.[2] Rather, they were Puritans in their theology and regular human beings with unique personalities, strengths, struggles, interests, backgrounds, and accomplishments. They grappled with the same questions others of their age (and ours) sought to answer. In some ways they upheld the status quo of gender roles, but in other ways they challenged and even outright rejected it; they suffered from injustice but also found ways to fulfill their life callings in spite of the societal restrictions placed on them. In fact, I would describe the women in the following chapters as strong-willed and bold, much more than I am, a millennial living in Vancouver with four university degrees and zero kids. Their stories inspire me to be more confident, grounded, and resilient, and less self-conscious, complaisant, and fragile. Regardless of whether or not we agree with them on every point, the fact is, they deserve to be studied just like any other group of women from the past. And, though this has not always been the case, they deserve to be interpreted with generosity, not disdain. Reading their words as they intended—for example, as Lucy Hutchinson termed one of her writings a "testimony of . . . love"—is simply doing good history.[3]

More than this, Puritan women are valuable subjects of study for believers today—you and me—because they had great insight into the Christian life and good instincts regarding matters of human relationships. This is partly because the Puritans as a whole stand out in church history for being particularly skilled at applying the Bible to all areas of existence, making them some of the best figures to consult on various topics of Christian living even hundreds of years later. As Packer said, they had a spiritual maturity—"a compound of wisdom, goodwill, resilience, and creativity"—that was born out of hardship and is often lacking in our time of "ease and luxury."[4] And, I would add, Puritan women frequently wrote about aspects of daily life, thus revealing to us what their relationships with God, family, church, and society were really like—the good, the bad, the ugly, and also the beautiful. As Mary Rich said about the godly women in her time, they may have looked "plain" on the outside, but they were "velvet within."[5]

Thus, this book seeks to retell the stories of five Puritan women as they told them—rather than as we might have expected or wanted them to be told—in order to appreciate who they really were. By doing this, it is my hope that we will not only learn about them but also learn about ourselves, foster a sense of comradery among Christian women today, and open our minds to the existence of other women who deserve to be studied. Now you may be asking, "Isn't this a book about Puritan women, not other women today or in the past?" Yes. But there are some wonderful ripple effects of such a study.

First, by reading their stories, we will be able to better interpret our own stories, because—as the novel-readers, artist-lovers, and movie-goers of the world will tell you—there are lessons that cannot be learned (or at least are hard to learn) from direct instruction. Sometimes, it is only when we take a step back from our lives and enter the life of another person—messy and complex as it always is—that we are able to gain the perspective needed to think creatively about our own greatest problems and deepest desires, especially as they relate to the people we love most in this world. More than this, because their stories are true, real-life ones, reading them drums into our brains that God is in control and we will be okay. Seeing the spiritual success of women in church history is like seeing a science experiment done over and over again with different variables but the same results—it shows us that yes, it can be done! You can get through heartache, slander, illness, the death of a loved one, war, anything, because so many women, filled with the Holy Spirit, have already done it.

Further, I hope that Christian women who read this book will be encouraged to see themselves as part of a whole, that is, all women of the Christian faith. The reason I think this is especially valuable right now is because the topic of gender roles has become so volatile and divisive that it has wearied half of the church and turned sisters into strangers, even enemies. Though these debates are often conducted by male theologians and biblical scholars, it is usually women—both egalitarians and complementarians—who end up bearing the emotional burden of the debates. Having who you are as a person constantly discussed by other people in a contentious way can make you feel on edge about your own identity. These debates can also pit us against each other by making a secondary theological issue seem like the most important issue to you because you are included in the debated topic, thus permanently separating you from those on the other side.

So what does this have to do with reading about Puritan women? In my experience, I've found that one way to counteract the negative effects of these debates about gender is to celebrate how God used all sorts of women in the past to build up his church. What happened in history happened, whether we like it or not; the women who existed in history existed, whether they were who we hoped they would be or not. And it is these real women from the actual past—who came from various backgrounds, held to different theological convictions, made mistakes, and dealt with gender controversies of their own time—that passed on the faith to the next generation. Christian women have so much more to share with each other than they have to fight about, and I hope this book can help us embrace that fact and thus develop a deeper appreciation and respect for each other as well as a sense of connection with our spiritual heritage.

Finally, by reading about Puritan women, we not only gain an understanding of who they were as a group, but also get a taste of the vast contributions of women throughout church history. You see, not all women were exactly the same—not even these five Puritan women, who had much in common. This means that the more we read women's writings with our own eyes, the more our minds will be opened to the existence of lots of other women, who did lots of different things and wrote about lots of different things! So, in this book you will not only meet a handful of Christians who lived over four-hundred years ago but also be prompted to consider how half of God's people have built up the church in ways that we may have not noticed before. If this is the first time you're reading about women in church history, I expect it will not be the last.

Five Women, Five Homes

Thus, it is with barefaced advocacy and the hope of sparking a reading revival that the following chapters visit the homes of five Puritan women while they ministered to their families. As mothers, daughters, grandmothers, and wives, these women discipled their loved ones by using spiritual practices that enabled them to devote themselves to God and bring his word to bear upon their family members' hearts. But before setting out on this adventure, one that will take us to England, America, and back, I would like to make sure you understand why we are highlighting their use of spiritual practices, visiting them at home, and looking at specific family relationships.

The first is the most obvious: these women were mature and effective believers *because* they devoted themselves to God using spiritual practices. In the following pages, I focus on a specific practice that each woman implemented in her life because it naturally comes to the forefront of her writings, but it is important to remember that these were not the only practices they used. For example, Brilliana Harley not only talked with others about spiritual things but also prayed (like Anne Bradstreet), studied theology (like Lucy Hutchinson), and donated to charity (like Mary Rich). This use of many practices and the overlapping of each one on top of another shows us that Christian living is characterized by integrity: it functions not in compartmentalized segments, but as a whole life (every aspect of your existence) and whole person (every aspect of your being) endeavor. Their reading of Scripture, attending church services, and caring for others were all intertwined. As they played one melody, they were led to add another harmony, creating a symphony of devotion and service that we call the Christian life.

Second, I have chosen to peer into their relationships with family centered in the home simply because this was one of the primary places where they applied their use of spiritual practices to daily Christian living and wrote about it. For this same reason I also highlight a specific relationship that takes center stage in each of their unique writings, though we'll also see them acting as sisters, cousins, aunts, and mothers-in-law. However, as I mentioned earlier, these women were by no means confined to the home but were involved in many other aspects of society, like education, business, medicine, and politics.[6] And, of course, even when they were at home, this did not mean they weren't working, as "housewifery was itself a skilled, consuming, and labour-intensive occupation."[7] Thus, though their spiritual writings are set in the context of their family life, that was not the only thing they had going on, and it may not have looked like you think it did.

More than this, learning from these women as children, spouses, parents, and grandparents by no means makes them irrelevant to orphaned, widowed, divorced, or infertile believers today. In fact, each woman in this book experienced the unexpected death of a family member; some lost a spouse, others a parent, a child, and even a grandchild. Similarly, these women did not necessarily have stable housing situations—living in one place of peace and quiet—but faced significant disruptions, with some inheriting property, others moving around, and the rest having their homes sold or destroyed. Thus, as much as this book is about having a family and a home, it is also about losing them.

Most importantly, not all of the women in the following chapters had a spouse or child during the time of our stories, for a significant portion of their lives, or ever, but they were always part of another very important family—the church. Since the church is a spiritual family (a theological point made explicitly by Lucy Hutchinson and clearly exhibited in the socially active lives of Mary Rich and Brilliana Harley), the ministry of these women can easily apply to those who may not have a large household but are still a part of God's home. So, if your biological family is small, has suffered separation or loss, does not own a nice house, or is just not what you hoped it would be, keep reading. These stories are for you as much as they are for any other readers. They show real families—biological and spiritual—in real homes, not perfect, pretend families protected by a white picket fence.

We will start our visits in England at the small village of Edworth, Bedfordshire, with young Agnes Beaumont as she testifies in a barn, her childhood home, and before a jury about her experiences of communing with God and evangelizing her father during a crisis. By reading her record of these events, we will discover how this new convert found the grit needed to defend Christianity in a winsome way and defend her own innocence with sincere humility.

Then, we will travel to some unknown spot between Owthorpe and London, where Lucy Hutchinson, advancing in age and diminishing in financial stability, is drafting a theological treatise—the only one of its kind written by a woman in her time—for her newlywed daughter Barbara. Here, we will find out why she went to such lengths to pass on the faith during the hardest period of her life when she could have simply sent Barbara an affordable catechism written by a professional theologian.

Afterward, we will head to the mansion of Mary Rich, the Countess of Warwick in the idyllic Leigh's Priory of Felsted, Essex. As we join her for a walk in the woods on her estate, we will see how she endured never-ending days with an ailing, angry husband and became inspired to help others weather even worse hardships, turning her story not just into one of survival but also great triumph.

Then, we will make the dangerous trek across the Atlantic Ocean to North Andover, Massachusetts, visiting Anne Bradstreet in one of her rustic American houses after her emigration from England and several moves within New England. Inside, Anne pens prayers in the form of poems for her ever-growing family and will show us how they mourned six consecutive losses without losing their faith in a good God or stifling their true emotions.

Crossing the ocean again, we will end up in the castle of Lady Brilliana Harley as she defends it against a siege and scribbles down letters to her son Edward. Though they may seem to be just words written on a page, Harley used such letters to creatively provide not only for Edward but also for their extended family and community, keeping everyone together in spirit at a time when civil war threatened to tear them apart.

Finally, after visiting each of their homes to hear their unique stories, we will bring them all into one room to have a conversation with each other and with us about their family ministry.

In my own story, I have seen again and again how God providentially uses whatever I'm currently reading to teach me a specific lesson or give me a specific comfort I desperately need at that exact moment. I hope (even expect!) that the same will happen to you as you encounter the writings of these fellow believers who came before you and recorded their testimonies of love not only for their earthly families but also for their spiritual family—including you.

1

Agnes Beaumont

Daughter as Evangelist, Using Memorization

WHEN TWENTYSOMETHING Agnes Beaumont (*bap.* 1652, *d.* 1720) got to her home in Edworth, Bedfordshire, England, late one Friday night, she was in big trouble—so much trouble, that her father, a single parent, would not let her enter the house until she promised to never do what she had done again. However, she was also strong-willed and would not agree to his terms. So that night, she slept outside in the barn, thinking about what she had done and wishing she was tucked in her warm bed. Certainly, she thought, this was a harsh punishment. But it was nothing compared to what would happen over the next several days as she was put on trial before a doctor, coroner, and jury. Her very life depended on a declaration of innocence. Amazingly, this country girl's own record of her trial has survived to this day and is considered "a rare example of [a conversion narrative] at this social level in the seventeenth century."[1] So, you ask, what exactly did she do?

Beaumont the New Convert

What initially got Beaumont kicked out of the house that fateful night was not what we might think a girl in her early twenties would do to rebel. Though it wasn't anything indecent, people had accused her of something that was, and the gossip of her supposed misbehavior spread all the way around town. What she actually did was get a ride to church with John Bunyan, the popular Baptist pastor who was preaching at a church in the nearby town of Gamlingay.

You see, Beaumont was a new convert to Christianity and a new member of this church; in fact, her name was the first one written into the membership book by Bunyan himself.[2] And like any new believer, she had a fervent zeal for God and godliness, so much so that when the man who was supposed to take her to church one morning did not show up, she convinced her brother (who would be taking his wife on their horse and didn't have room for another) to earnestly plead for a ride from the next passerby. It happened to be Bunyan. He initially refused, knowing her father was weary of her listening to his preaching. But Beaumont had so been looking forward to communing with God in the Lord's Supper that tears began to stream down her cheeks, and her brother, seeing her desperation, proclaimed, "If you do not carry her, you will break her heart."[3] Bunyan, who was often the subject of gossip and had only recently been released from a twelve-year imprisonment, was probably not in the mood for stirring up controversy and refused again, saying her father would be angry. This time,

Beaumont worked up the courage to speak for herself: "If you please to carry me, I will venture that."[4] It worked! Beaumont was on her way, and she could not be happier, exclaiming, "Oh, how glad was I that I was going."[5]

Her father, however, did not feel the same. Though she had managed to convince him to let her go to the service, he became enraged and chased after her (though he didn't catch up) once he realized who she was riding with. His strong dislike of Bunyan was partly because Bunyan was seen as a controversial, even dangerous, figure. Though he did not actually commit any of the egregious sins he was accused of, Baptists in general at this time were seen as a subversive group that threatened shared national values like the traditional family structure, a cornerstone of English society, and were often accused of "heresy, political rebellion, murder, sexual licence, and madness."[6] Thus, "contemporary fears about Baptist behaviour were deeply entrenched and could provoke extreme measures," so that "members of Beaumont's wider community had little difficulty in believing that she was a distracted fanatic, held in the thrall of a lascivious minister."[7] It seems Beaumont herself was aware of these stereotypes, as she went out of her way at the beginning of her narrative to show she was not a crazy woman. Though some had asked her if she was suicidal after seeing her crying a lot, she explained that her tears were "for joy and not for grief," a common experience in conversion.[8]

Thus, with nightmares of Bunyan and Baptists filling their heads, the townsfolk took notice of Beaumont as she rode past them. One man went so far as to start rumors of sexual impropriety between Bunyan and Beaumont.[9] Yet, the sin Beaumont admitted to was far from anything like fornication. As she recorded how happy she was to be going to the church service, she noted,

> But to speak the truth I had not gone far behind [Mr. Bunyan] when my heart was puffed up with pride, and I began to have high thoughts of myself, and proud to think I should ride behind such a man as he was; and I was pleased that anybody did look after me as I rode along. And sometimes he would be speaking to me about the things of God as we went along. And indeed I thought myself a happy body that day; first that it did please God to make way for my going to the meeting, and then that I should have the honor to ride behind him.[10]

It seems that Beaumont's only wrongdoing was being excited to talk to and be associated with her favorite preacher—not exactly grounds for a scandal.

At the church service, Beaumont got exactly what she was hoping for. She wrote, "Oh, it was a feast of fat things to me! My soul was filled with consolation. . . . Oh, I had such a sight of Jesus Christ that it broke my heart to pieces. . . . A sense of my sins, and of his dying love, made me love him, and long to be with him."[11] In fact, this particular service, she would later recall, was a special mercy to her because Jesus knew the trials she was about to endure and gave her "new manifestations of his love" at just the right time.[12]

Hussy

Since no one was returning past her house after the service, Beaumont had to walk back most of the way that night, "ploshing through the dirt" and fearing that she would not make it there before her father went to sleep.[13] When she arrived, her fears were confirmed, and she had to call through his bedroom window to wake him up, saying "Pray will you let me in; I am come home wet and dirty."[14] But her father, having stewed in his anger for most of the day, said she could never enter the house again unless she promised to not follow Bunyan anymore.

Beaumont did not know what to do. What happened to her in this moment of decision shows where her heart truly lay and what would carry her through much worse later on. She began to think of Bible passages she had memorized and decided to sleep outside in order to seek God's guidance. She recalled,

> I stood awhile at the window [to my father's bedroom] silent, and that consideration came to my mind, "What if I should come at last when the door is shut and Jesus Christ should say to me, 'Depart from me, I know you not'" [Matt. 7:21–23]. And it was secretly put into my mind to spend the night in prayer. . . . But these thoughts presently darted in upon my mind, "No, go to your brother's; there you may have a good supper and a warm bed, and the night is long and cold." "No," said I, "I will go, and cry to heaven for mercy for my soul, and for some new discoveries of the love of Christ."[15]

At first, she began to give in to her fears, thinking she might be attacked or die from the cold. But then she thought of two Bible passages, Matthew 6:6 and Psalm 50:15, which promise that your heavenly Father will see and reward you if you pray to him in secret, that he will answer and show you mighty things if you pray. So tired, dirty, and frightened, Beaumont went to the barn to pray the night away.

She did not regret it. In her words, that evening would become "a night to be remembered to my life's end."[16] Though she was at first scared and frozen, God calmed her heart, and she felt no cold. From hour to hour she prayed, praised, gave thanks to God, and meditated on various scriptural passages. One word that kept repeating in her mind was "beloved" from 1 Peter 4:12. She recalled, "[It] made such a melody in my heart, I cannot tell you," and as she lamented the loss of her earthly father's love she remembered that her heavenly father loved her.[17]

"Beloved" spoke louder than her fears and helped her face them the next morning when she reapproached her father, whose anger she had usually run away from in the past. Unfortunately, nothing had changed: either she stop going to these church meetings for the rest of her life or remain outside. At this point, Beaumont sought the help of other family members. First, her brother tried to reason with their father but got an even harsher response. Then, her sister-in-law tried to reason with him, but he upped the ante by threatening to leave his inheritance to someone he didn't know and to never give Beaumont a penny. He wouldn't even let her collect her Bible and paintings from inside the house.

Again, Beaumont was completely open about her spiritual weaknesses and admitted that it was hard for her to hear this. She began to wonder, "What will become of me?"[18] Now, she had an even tougher decision to make, as her commitment to attending church had the potential for much graver consequences than sleeping outside for one night. But again, she was reminded of Scripture—particularly Psalm 27:10, which says that "My father and mother have forsaken me, but the LORD will take me in"—and she stood her ground.

That night, she tried again to convince her father, thinking that he would need someone to make his dinner since she had been caring for him ever since her mother died when she was ten years old. This time, things only escalated. She found the house key in the door and took it, trying to get inside, but her father blocked the door, grabbed her, and threatened to throw her in the pond if she didn't give it back.

Yet, while she must have been shaken up, Beaumont continued to pray and think about Scripture, and she resolved to not give in. Her brother also sought to strengthen her will by telling her, "You are now brought upon the stage to act for Christ and his ways . . . I would not have you consent to my father upon his terms."[19] She even went to the church meeting the next day, though she was understandably nervous, and afterward made a final, clever effort to persuade her father, reasoning:

Father . . . I will serve you in anything that lies in me to do for you as long as you live and I live. . . . Father . . . I desire time to go nowhere but to hear God's word, if you will but let me go on Sabbath days to the meeting; and I desire no more. . . . Father . . . you can't answer for my sins, nor stand in my stead before God; I must look to the salvation of my soul, or I am undone forever.[20]

But, as her father held out the key with his terms for the last time and called her "hussy," she faltered and went back on her word, "Peter like."[21] As she stepped inside the house, she thought of two more passages, but they did not hold messages of comfort. Matthew 10:33 and 37 reminded her that Christ said, "Whoever denies me before men, I also will deny before my Father who is in heaven," and "Whoever loves father or mother more than me is not worthy of me." As she made her father dinner and tried to sleep, Beaumont was haunted by these words. The next day was no better; she waited for her father to leave the house so she could cry freely and didn't say much to her brother because she felt ashamed. Overall, it seemed like she was in a worse position than before. The only thing that got her through the day was contemplating Luke 22:31, which records that Satan desired to take Simon but Jesus prayed for him, and 1 Corinthians 10:13, which says that God will "provide [a] way of escape." Drawing some hope from these passages, she pleaded with God to change her father's mind and asked God to forgive her.

Beloved

Though she tried to hide her tears, Beaumont's father noticed that she was in distress and asked what was wrong, and she explained her regret. Shockingly, after two days straight of treating her harshly, even to the point of verbal and physical abuse, her father "wept like a child."[22] He said he did not want to disagree with her and had worried about her the first night she was gone, though he thought she had slept at her brother's house. He explained that someone in town had told him horrible things about Bunyan, even though he had, in the past, heard Bunyan preach "with a broken heart" and was even led to pray.[23] Further, Beaumont's radical conversion had troubled him because she had become so zealous but he himself "scarce ever thought of [his] soul."[24] Beaumont's efforts had finally paid off, and reconciliation had begun. The next night, after her father was asleep, she sat up and prayed that God would save him and be near her in the coming week. Like her times of prayer before, she said this was "a very sweet season to my poor soul," and she went to bed happy.[25]

But in the middle of the night, she woke up to a "doleful noise" coming from her father, who was having heart pain.[26] Fearing for his life, he began to call out to God, saying "Lord . . . have mercy on me. I am a poor miserable sinner; Lord Jesus, wash me in your precious blood."[27] Beaumont ran to him and prayed with him, which, she said, was "more than ever I did with him before."[28] Then, using her skill of looking at the heart and speaking to it (as she had done earlier for her own soul), she said, "Father . . . there is mercy in Jesus Christ for sinners. Lord help you to lay hold of it," and he confessed, "Oh . . . I have been against you for seeking after Jesus Christ; the Lord forgive me and lay not that sin to my charge."[29]

At this point, he began to rapidly wane and was soon unresponsive. Beaumont was convinced she needed to get help. Crying out to God and remembering Isaiah 41:10, which says to not be afraid because he will help you, she confronted her fears about running to her brother's house at night and took off in the dark, the snow accumulating and melting in her shoes so that they fell off along the way. When fears of being attacked assaulted her mind again, she combated them with Psalm 34:7, which says that "the angel of the LORD encamps around those who fear him." She finally arrived, and her yelling startled the entire household—they could not even recognize her voice or properly clothe themselves due to the scare of being awakened in the night but soon ran back to her house together.

That night, Beaumont's father died. She was crushed, but "had some hopes [her] father was gone to heaven notwithstanding."[30] She was also led to think of her own death and asked God for comfort that she too would go to heaven when the time came, after which she remembered Isaiah 35:10, which promises that "the ransomed of the LORD shall return and come to Zion with singing; everlasting joy shall be upon their heads; they shall obtain gladness and joy, and sorrow and sighing shall flee away." In her grief, she again thought of the word "beloved" and determined that God had turned the bad events of the past few days into good, despite the hurt and loss.

Maiden

Certainly, Beaumont had been through enough. At this point, she should have been given the time to properly mourn the death of her father with her family and friends and begin the slow process of recovering from so much trauma in so little time. But she would only now come to her final test. To understand this test, we must briefly go back in time. Prior to all of this controversy, a lawyer in town named Mr. Feery had wanted Beaumont to marry his son and thus influenced her father's will so that he would leave his daughter with more money than he had originally planned. However, it seems that after Beaumont had turned to the dark side of the Baptists, Feery no longer wanted anything to do with her and now set out for revenge.[31] Approaching Beaumont's brother the night after their father died, Feery made an outlandish accusation: he suspected that Beaumont had murdered her father with poison she got from Bunyan. Offended and amazed, but seeing Feery was determined to follow through on his suspicion, Beaumont's brother agreed to an investigation. He went home, and after telling his wife, they were both in great distress and spent the night bringing everything to God before telling Beaumont the next day.

Needless to say, she was also shocked and disturbed. Not only was her reputation on the line but also the reputation of her beloved pastor, who had already gone through so much, and even the reputation of God, who they represented to a watching world. Yet, she did find some comfort in the fact that she had a clear conscience. And soon, with such little warning, her official trial began.

She was first questioned by a doctor. He did not find any proof but was pressured by Feery to continue the investigation and thus told Beaumont's brother they would need to get a coroner and jury. Now, things were getting serious. Beaumont may have even felt the many Baptist stereotypes weighing on her as she was accused of committing the most heinous assault on the family structure that her society could imagine. In her day, murdering one's father was considered petty treason, punishable by burning at the stake. Naturally, this terrified her! She wrote, "I see my life lay at the stake," and "Thoughts of burning would sometimes shake me to pieces."[32] But, just as in every trial before, more scriptural passages ran through her mind, this time, Isaiah 54:17 and 43:2, which promise that "no weapon that is fashioned against you shall succeed, . . . you shall refute every tongue that rises against you in judgment," and God will be with you when you go through the fire. Now, she thought, even if she were tortured to death, God would give her his presence in that moment. So she entrusted herself to her Lord, knowing she was his in life or death, and prayed that his name would not suffer.

Before the coroner arrived to question Beaumont, her friends from church came to her brother's house to pray for her, and she also took time to pray privately. Again, like all the times before, she drew strength from God's closeness. Her only hope was that she would not now hang her head in shame before the "company of . . . carnal men" that she would testify in front of but be confident of her own innocence and even "look [her] accuser in the face with boldness."[33] As her father's lifeless body lay near her, she remembered Job 17:9, which says "the righteous holds to his way, and he who has clean hands grows stronger and stronger." Then, one by one, the jury members and coroner viewed the body, and the questioning began.

However, it was not Beaumont who struggled to answer—it was Feery. Not only did he have to be located and brought to the trial when he didn't arrive on time, but he couldn't give any concrete proof to support his accusation, merely saying that Beaumont and her father had gotten into a fight a few days before his death. In the end, the coroner rebuked Feery, declaring,

> You that have defamed this maid after this manner, you had needs make it your business now to repair her reputation again. You have taken away her good name from her, and you would have taken away her life from her if you could. She met with enough I think. . . . If you should have given her five hundred pounds, it would not make her amends.[34]

This swiftly put an end to the trial. Yet, despite such a public and conclusive affirmation of Beaumont's innocence, Feery's rumor was revived a month later and people began to believe that she had since confessed to poisoning her father. In a final act of courage, bolstered by the scriptures in her mind and times of communion with God, Beaumont held her head high and ventured into the marketplace to show she was no longer disturbed by the gossip and that God's name had not been brought to shame. She remembered Matthew 5:11–12, which argues that you are blessed when people "revile you and persecute you and utter all kinds of evil against you falsely on [God's] account." And as she passed through the crowds, feeling every eye on her and hearing snickers, she thought, "Oh . . . mock on, there is a day a coming [that] will clear all."[35]

After all of this, the most shocking part of Beaumont's story is how she ends it in writing, "Thus I have told you of the good and evil things that I met with in that dispensation. I wish I was well in my soul as I was then."[36]

Agnes

Beaumont's story has so many surprises. How a young woman who was a new convert endured such troubles back-to-back is impressive, and we may rightly wonder how she did it. Perhaps the key is found in a line that is repeated over and over in her narrative—that scriptures suddenly "came into," "ran mightily through," "darted upon," or "dropped upon" her mind.[37] She did not have a physical Bible with her in these instances. Her recollection of passages occurred in moments of decision when she had to think on her feet and act quickly, and it was through memorization that she was able to act out of faith instead of fear.

While we might think of this practice as cold and methodical, Beaumont's story shows us that it led her to experiences of intimate communion with God, a closeness to him that would carry her through each hardship and make an imprint on her soul, thus shaping her instincts according to who she was when she was with him. And it was because of this intimacy not just with Scripture but with God himself that Beaumont was able to be balanced in situations that can only be described as extreme, mature in situations that were anything but simple.

Though it seemed the world, and even her own father, were doing everything they could to set her desire to love God at odds with her desire to love people, she strove to be simultaneously bold in the faith and at peace with those who did not share it. She knew her father was not right with God, but she did not throw this in his face when they had a disagreement about church. Rather, she appealed to whatever sense of respect he did have for Christianity and tried to fulfill her responsibilities to both him and God, attempting to bring them together instead of tear them further apart. Perhaps her moderateness and reasonableness are exactly what made her father realize she had not gone crazy or been brainwashed; perhaps her weaving together of faith and family is what made her witnessing to her father while he was dying so effective. She had shown herself to be calm, exhibited her faith before him in word and deed, and did not give up on trying to reconcile, so when he was prompted to humble himself and repent before her, he probably felt reassured. Here, with his own daughter, he was speaking to someone who not only had a similar repenting experience—one where emotions ran high and tears flowed—but also someone who knew and loved God, and even someone who knew and loved him.

We may want to question some of Beaumont's decisions (like sleeping in the barn instead of going to her brother's and eventually giving in to her father's demands) or even believe she was a bit crazy like the townsfolk said. But this would be sacrificing a great thing for something only potentially mediocre. Beaumont may have been considered odd—even base—by others, but she was willing to do what she believed was required of her to be a faithful Christian and child. Can we say the same of ourselves? Or would we rather be thought of as sophisticated, sporting a polished public appearance in our community instead of risking our reputation for religion? Being zealous and having a concern for those around us who do not share such zeal may make our relationships feel a bit awkward or get us accused of hanging out with sinners. But, as Beaumont showed, it's possible, and it's worth it—you may never know how much. What if Beaumont hadn't gone to church that fateful day, or if she didn't do everything in her power to reconcile with her father? I hope that, like her, we won't ever have cause to wonder what would have happened if we had done our best to worship God and live in harmony with others.

Similarly, Beaumont also found a balance in being patient when she was falsely accused (several times!) while also defending her innocence. In a later copy of her narrative, a note was added to record yet *another* rumor started by Feery the next year about Beaumont setting a house on fire, and it may be that these many rumors are part of why she did not marry until middle age and seemed to never have children.[38] But we can imagine that, just like her testifying in court and strolling in the market, she held her head high, knowing she was innocent. Instead of seeking revenge or completely losing all hope or doubting her own self-worth even when the gossip was embarrassing and horrendous, Beaumont waited for the right time, place, and audience to tell the truth. And, unfortunately for Feery, that happened to not only be the doctor, coroner, and jury at her trial, but eventually her entire surrounding community, as she wrote everything down in this narrative, which we know—from the existence of later copies like the one mentioned above—was read and passed around.[39]

Perhaps most importantly, Beaumont found a balance between freely admitting her sin and yet always being confident in her relationship with God, knowing he was full of mercy and her identity was secure. This was a girl who understood salvation. When Beaumont committed a transgression—sometimes small (like feeling proud to be seen with Bunyan) and sometimes bigger (like promising to not go to church)—she completely opened her heart to show whatever ugliness hid there. Then, she reminded herself of passages that showed how merciful God is to the repentant and asked him to give her a way out. Though she did not assume she was a true believer based on zero evidence (clearly, she loved God, studied his word, was committed to worshiping with his people, cared for her family, and shunned wrongdoing), she also did not brush off her sin too quickly. She simply called it out for what it was, brought it to God, and asked him for forgiveness and help. Others may have labeled her a crazy woman, a whore, or a murderer, but she knew that God labeled her his beloved.

Never losing her love for the church and its ministers, Beaumont would go on to financially contribute to a new building for the Tilehouse Street Baptist meeting in Hitchin—a secret congregation that Bunyan had helped establish—and "was buried at her own request near the [persecuted] minister John Wilson" in the church yard.[40] And, though we may read the record of her trial and hope we never have to go what she went through, she herself concluded the entire story by saying it was during this time that her soul felt the most whole. So don't despair of the trials in your life and think everything is going to be better once they're over; God is with you now, and being close to him is the best thing you can experience in this life or the next. May we all confess with Beaumont,

Oh, the great consolations and enlargements of heart, with fervent desires after Jesus Christ and his grace, which have often made me thank God for trouble when I have found it drive me nearer to himself and to the throne of grace. . . . Oh, it cannot be expressed with tongue what sweetness there is in one promise of God when he is pleased to apply it to the soul by his Spirit. It turns sorrow into joy, fears into faith; it turns weeping and mourning into rejoicing, which, blessed be God, I have experienced these things and many more.[41]

2

Lucy Hutchinson

Mother as Theologian, Using Fellowship

IT IS NOT OFTEN that a child has to convince a parent to go
to church, like Agnes Beaumont did; usually, it's the other way
around, and parents know all too well the cunning methods
they've sometimes used to drag their children out of the house
on Sundays. What lengths have you gone to make sure your
children, your nieces and nephews, or your friend's offspring stay
connected to the church as they grow up? Perhaps you've prayed
for them or coaxed them to spend time with other church kids.
Maybe you've had to carry them to services, kicking and scream-
ing, enacted some form of grounding until they agreed to attend,
or even bribed them!

For Lucy Hutchinson (1620–1681), a mother of eight in England, making sure her newlywed daughter Barbara remained a
part of the church was so important that she decided to write an
entire theological treatise for her. If this sounds extreme to you,

make it even more extreme, for we have no other document like this in the seventeenth century written by a woman; it is truly one of a kind.[1] Just as Beaumont's narrative is unique because of her social status, so is Hutchinson's treatise for its combination of genre and gender—a woman writing theology.

Hutchinson the Intellectual

But that raises the question, why *didn't* women write technical theological works at this time? One of the underlying reasons was that, sadly, girls were not educated in the same way that boys were in the seventeenth century. While their brothers were prepared for school and then (if they came from a well-to-do family) received a formal education at university, sisters were prepared for marriage and thus learned skills that would be required for running a household. Though girls could learn other subjects at home and schools for girls did exist, engagement with the academic world was not a part of their typical upbringing as females.[2]

Yet, little Lucy turned out to be too nerdy for this path. From a young age, she was not interested in "girl" subjects and proved to be better at what the boys were learning. As she later recalled about her childhood, she would memorize sermons that she heard, "absolutely hated" sewing, used every moment possible to read books, and found ways to ditch playmates her own age so that she could listen to the interesting things that the adults in the house were talking about.[3] Instead of squelching her passion, her parents recognized such natural talent and supported her, with her father arranging for her to be tutored in more diverse subjects at home and her mother taking her to sermons, ultimately inspiring in Lucy a love of theology as the greatest of all subjects that could be studied. Eventually, Lucy became proficient in Latin, poetry, and theology, overall proving to be "an immensely talented female intellectual" who "successfully laid claim to an education" that was in her time normally restricted to men.[4]

In fact, when Lucy attracted a suitor, it was her book collection that first impressed him. When John Hutchinson, escorted by Lucy's sister, visited their house and found out that a stack of Latin books belonged to Lucy, he became immediately interested in meeting her. Though she was self-admittedly a recluse, preferring to study rather than visit with people, she found John to be "advantageably conversed with," and they immediately became friends and soon fiancés.[5] As a married couple, they spent their days studying Scripture, debating theological questions with local pastors, listening to sermons, and catechizing their children, providing both their daughters and sons with a comprehensive education. Lucy herself would go on to write and translate several works of poetry, theology, and history, skillfully interacting with the ideas of brainiacs like John Owen.[6] And though it hasn't been given much credit, one of Lucy's best writing accomplishments was her *Principles of the Christian Religion*, wherein she shows herself to be a theologian in her own right, using her knowledge and skill to give the best of herself to her daughter Barbara right in the middle of the most difficult period of her own life.

Profoundly Unfeminine

In the years leading up to writing this theology book, Hutchinson went through a series of unfortunate events. First, her husband was arrested for his involvement in the parliamentarian cause, which had opposed and then executed King Charles I in the English Civil

Wars.[7] Hutchinson herself had also been highly involved in this cause, keeping a record of local events and serving as a nurse who cared not only for her own soldiers but also those on the other side when the need arose. Yet, the parliamentarians' plans were thwarted by the restoration of King Charles II to the throne, who then began to seek justice for the death of his father. Overall, the failure of this dream for a godly England (wherein true worship and upright governance would be restored in the nation) was nothing short of devastating for many Puritans—mentally, financially, and socially.

It was also devastating on an even more personal level for Hutchinson, as John would soon die in prison. At that moment, her whole life changed. Without him, she was left to care for their children—one of whom was "mortally ill"—and try to finance their educations while also paying off his debts of £9,000.[8] This led her to eventually sell off her estates and attempt to find employment for her kids.[9] Though she was not destitute, it felt like she had lost everything—a full and happy life with her family in what was supposed to be a restored homeland.[10]

On top of these exceptional circumstances, Hutchinson's intellectual pursuits were also hampered by limitations placed on all women at the time. For example, women did not typically have a room or desk reserved to do work that was outside of the norm, so it is probable that Hutchinson's workspace was anything but conducive to deep theological thought.[11] Further, female authors were often praised for being pious but scolded for being knowledgeable, as "many writers of the period . . . deplored learning in women, seeing it as a worldly preoccupation all too likely to distract them from the spiritual and domestic concerns more appropriate to a woman's place in life."[12]

Thus, though Hutchinson's memoirs of her husband would become her most popular book and receive praise for mentioning John more than herself, her *Principles of the Christian Religion*, which only mentions him once, was viewed as "profoundly unfeminine" and "fell into obscurity."[13] As David Norbrook aptly puts it, a Lucy Hutchinson who wrote theology "was not the Lucy Hutchinson that readers wanted."[14]

In light of all this, it is not surprising to find Hutchinson opening Barbara's book by referencing the many factors that conspired against her to make writing it difficult. Though her theological writings reveal a "relative lack of concern for conventional ideals of womanly conduct," it is clear that the pressures placed on her as a mother and a woman took an emotional toll.[15] She wrote to Barbara, "My infirmities and imperfections joined with my outward ill successes have much weakened my authority," and "I have had many distractions of spirit and interruptions in setting down these things."[16] But Hutchinson, toughened by her years of being a nurse and seeing her husband waste away in prison, dug her heels in and determined, "Yet I cannot be wanting to my duty . . . [and] proceed with so many clogs upon me."[17]

Your Truly Affectionate Mother

Thus, when Hutchinson wrote the only theological treatise we have from a woman at this time, she was not lounging around, contemplating deep thoughts in peace—she was sick, strung out, and feeling like a failure. But she knew the importance of ensuring the spiritual stability of her daughter and pressed forward in her unconventional ambition. As previously mentioned, Hutchinson said that she wrote this treatise so that Barbara—recently married and moving away to start an independent life as an adult—would not be seduced by religious factions to stray from the "catholic faith and universal love wherein all that are true Christians must unite."[18] Thus, Hutchinson drafted a summary of the essential doctrines of that faith, starting with knowledge of the triune God and his nature and then moving to discuss creation, salvation from sin, and right worship.

Strengthening the love bond between her daughter and the church was so important to Hutchinson because she believed it was a sin to separate from or cause divisions in the church. She explained:

> Sects are a great sin and Christians ought all to live in the unity of the spirit and though it cannot be but that offences will come in the church yet woe be to them by whom they come. . . . Love is the bond of perfectness and they that break the communion of saints walk not charitably and will be accountable to God for it. In his name therefore I beg of you to study and exercise universal love to every member of Christ under whichever denomination you find them.[19]

Thus, Hutchinson's passing on of the universal church's faith to Barbara was for the purpose of love. Of course, as a mother writing to her daughter, she expressed a special affection for Barbara, signing off and saying this document was

> a testimony of my best and most tender love to you who cannot consider the age and temptations you are cast upon without great thoughts of heart and earnest prayers for you many times

when you sleep and dream not of the spiritual loving care I have for you. I acknowledge your love to me and bless God for the good hopes he has given me of you and of your sincere love to him. . . . Your truly affectionate mother.[20]

Yet, more than this, Hutchinson believed it was her specific duty as a mother to write this treatise for Barbara. She was not willing to leave the fate of Barbara's relationship with the church in the hands of others or even just Barbara's but considered herself responsible. Hutchinson thus lays the blame at her own feet for "any attempts [that] have been made to shake" Barbara's faith and concludes,

> I know there are many sound and holy books I might commend to you which have collected these instructions more methodically . . . I know you may say you can read the word and make collections thence yourself . . . but when you do you will find it my duty to exhort and admonish you according to the talent entrusted with me. . . . The sense of my own duty carries me on in this work . . . to give you my light in Christian practice as well as in the doctrine of the faith.[21]

As we know from the story of her childhood, Hutchinson was not against books—she seemed to love them more than anything else! It would be equally odd to think she would be against Barbara reading a book herself. Thus, by writing her own treatise for Barbara, Hutchinson was not attempting to downplay the importance of academic qualifications or of personal study. Rather, she simply believed that basic theological education should be given by those who are responsible for the student's spiritual well-being. She admits that Barbara may not even want to receive her teaching and that in teaching Barbara herself she is not attempting to simply express her personal opinions (since she uses trustworthy sources like the Westminster Confession). But such ambition to instruct Barbara in her own words is legitimate because she is her mother and thus has a duty to teach just as Barbara has a duty to listen, since the substance of her teaching is from God's word and thus has his stamp of authority.

Yet, Hutchinson does not stop there. She not only sets out to teach Barbara but also encourages Barbara to do the same with her own "children and servants."[22] As seen in the "oral delivery" that Hutchinson's mother used to teach her as a child, this household discipleship did not have to be accomplished by writing long treatises.[23] Hutchinson also used this verbal method with her children before writing her treatise by keeping a notebook of bits and pieces of theology, Bible verses, and sermon notes that she used to "prepare herself for expounding doctrines to members of her household."[24] In fact, Hutchinson told Barbara, she actually learned more when she taught the foundations of the faith to others rather than when she simply read about them on her own.

Yet, Hutchinson's concern in her thelogy book for those outside her immediate family went even further, as seen when she explained that "if the Lord shall make me be able to declare what he has done for my soul I intend to communicate it, that what has fixed me may fix others also."[25] Here, she recalls how in the past she went through times of doubt but God kept her firm in the faith, and she now hopes that this experience would be used to encourage not only Barbara and her household but also people outside of these circles. In case you haven't yet realized, that means you and me! So if you weren't able to learn from your mom or dad, or you're looking for inspiration in teaching your own kids, you've come to the right place, as this truly affectionate mother is not only speaking to Barbara, but anyone else who wants to listen.

Brothers and Sisters in Christ

After making this initial connection between the church's faith and fellowship, Hutchinson started to more firmly lay its theological foundation, brick by brick. At the bottom of it all is how faith and love inherently work together. Hutchinson summarized, "The operations of faith are by love, which has two branches, the one to God and the other to our neighbor."[26] In other words, our faith in God leads to loving him and the people around us. But even underneath this—our faith in God—is God himself, for it is union with Christ by the Holy Spirit that allows believers to receive his benefits, including reconciliation, which Hutchinson defines as having "peace with God" and even "with all creatures."[27]

Thus, faith in Christ—who has brought reconciliation—naturally expresses itself in love. Though such love must begin with and be most eminent for God himself in that he first loves us and must be loved above all else, this love for God necessarily leads to a love for his people, especially those who reflect him best.[28] It also leads to a love for praising God with each other. In fact, Hutchinson reasoned, God is *more* glorified and believers *more* encouraged when they worship together. This encouragement received from corporate worship is so wonderful that it is best understood not by explaining it but by having an embodied experience of it yourself. Hutchinson wrote:

The society of Christians joining in his worship adds force to every spirit by the gathering of them together into the spirit of the Lord and makes the presence of the Lord among them more glorious and more joyful in such a manner as cannot be expressed but by them who have experienced it.[29]

These ideas about church fellowship are also found in Hutchinson's two personal statements of faith (written in her notebook), which may have been used to help her first think through the wording she would later employ in her lengthier treatise.[30] Here, she admitted that though the visible church contains both true believers and hypocrites, coming together is "so profitable, and delightful, that it is the duty of everyone to uphold it so far as they are able."[31] In other words, it is not just enjoyable to worship with fellow Christians but also necessary. Thus Hutchinson continued on to argue that believers are required to join a congregation that worships rightly, attend its public assemblies, and submit to its discipline.

But that isn't all. As much as Christians must worship properly, they must also do service properly, not only offering practical help to one another but also being ready to do whatever charity is required in society, like feeding the hungry, visiting the sick, and clothing the naked. Because it's easier to do these things when physically close, Hutchinson naturally suggests that Christians living in the same location should consider gathering together. She explained,

I think it very convenient for believers that live so near as that they by that neighborhood have opportunity should enter into a league with God and each other . . . watching over one another in love, exhorting, instructing, comforting, and reproving each other, and taking care of the good of their brother's souls as their own, blessing and magnifying the name of the Lord together and communicating all the gifts and graces they have received of him for the benefit of each other and the whole church.[32]

Precisely because of her definition of the church as an entity united in shared values and a shared life, Hutchinson went on to compare the church to a family. Like a family, the members of a church are imperfect people who have all sorts of quirks, embarrassing stories, and even sins. But they are so intimately connected and committed to each other that, even when some are acting out or not pulling their weight, they will not leave one another but reaffirm their unbreakable bond and persevere together. Thus, distancing herself from Christians in her time who were so caught up in inter-denominational debates that they neglected basic religious virtues, Hutchinson publicly proclaimed to her readers that all true believers "under whatever errors or weaknesses they be, I desire to own as brothers and sisters in Christ and to exercise toward them all offices of charity."[33]

Every Man and Woman in the World

Some critics believe this is where the love of the Puritan stopped—they merely accepted the people in their own families and their own churches, and only when such people complied with their strict rules of right behavior and belief. But I imagine Hutchinson—who had tended to the wounds of her enemies in the midst of war—would have laughed at this accusation. How absurd is it to think the love of God is confined! No. The love that Christians must show to one another in worshiping together, caring for each other, and not creating divisions or separating comes from God himself, who is infinite and extends his love to all human beings in particular ways. Thus, just as believers are to love those in the church because they are God's people, so must they love those outside the church because they are God's creation.

"But what about sin?" you ask. Well, Hutchinson would reply that sin does influence how we love unbelievers—but it also influences how we love all people. As she wrote to Barbara in her theological treatise, even though God's people must hate sin, including that of unbelievers, they must also love unbelievers as human beings created by God and even potentially repentant, hoping for and working toward their conversion. In fact, believers must not only hate sin in unbelievers but also sin in their families and their own hearts even *more* than they hate sin in others! In Hutchinson's words, loving God makes the Christian

> to hate all things that are contrary to his holiness, even in themselves and their most beloved relations. "Do not I hate" says David, "the workers of iniquity? I hate them with a perfect hatred" [Pss. 5:5; 139:21–22]. Yet saints hate them thus only as workers of iniquity; as men and creatures of God they love them so as to desire and endeavor their conversion, but they hate their sins, and those most that prevail in their own hearts and the hearts of those that are dearest to them.[34]

By admitting to the presence of indwelling sin in the hearts of loved ones and oneself, Hutchinson calls her readers to replace a reactive and clouded hatred of sin with a righteous and clear-sighted hatred. This means the Christian home must not be a place of pretend holiness, where real evil in the household is swept under the rug and sinners on the street are mocked or demonized beyond recognition, but a place of daily repentance and forgiveness that seeks to be fair in its evaluation of good and bad, no matter where—or in whom—it is found.

It is not surprising to find Hutchinson saying that the Christian's love for all people comes from God since she said the same about loving fellow believers. Yet, after making this point, Hutchinson shockingly reverses her regular sequence to say that sometimes believers are not thankful to God enough for the common graces he gives because of their lack of love for all people, and thus they should love them more in order to be more thankful to God. In other words, she not only made a qualitative connection between love of God and human beings by saying you cannot love God without loving people, but also a quantitative connection by saying the more you love people (in a healthy way) the more you will love God! Now do you see why I think Hutchinson would laugh at the accusation that the Puritans only loved their own?

And this isn't even all of it. When Hutchinson made this point, she used a metaphor often reserved as an image for the church, namely, the body, saying believers should view themselves as intimately connected to all people in their humanity and be more thankful for the fact that this whole body receives good gifts from God rather than just certain parts of the body. Her train of thought is best seen when taken all together in her own words. She told Barbara:

Common benefits [we receive from God] are commonly slighted or not taken notice of. While the whole world shares with us the glorious and admirable benefit of light, we seldom consider what cause of thanksgiving we have for that mercy, and so for the air, fire, water, summer, winter, and the like. And this is for want of humanity and love to mankind, for did we consider ourselves to be one body with them, we would be more thankful to God for imparting his benefit to all then if it were only particularly extended to ourselves, wherefore David stirs up his soul to praise God for his goodness to the children of men. This makes him in a holy ecstasy to admire the bounty of God to mankind when he says, "Lord what is man that you are mindful of him" [Ps. 8:4]. . . . The common benefits, which God of his unspeakable mercy and goodness extends to all the children of men, [are] so worthy of admiration.[35]

Thus, instead of excluding those on the outside of their spiritual family, believers are supposed to embrace them as family in another way—still calling them to and hoping for their repentance, but not withholding basic courtesy, comradery, and affection.

Hutchinson continued on, saying God not only blesses humanity with the elements and seasons, but also with his entire universe and the vast array of "glorious creatures" who have "such various and excellent virtues."[36] Hutchinson wanted to pay attention to, appreciate, and sanctify the created world around her, every aspect of human existence and every human being, because God's love is so great that it reaches every little bit of life and overflows in its abundance. Thus, she concluded this section of her book by bringing all of the wonder together to exclaim how intentional, universal, and extraordinary God's blessings to all people are by giving "particularly to every man and woman in the world" so that even those who "lie under the heaviest outward pressure have infinite cause of thanks."[37]

When Hutchinson had lost so much, including her husband, her house, her political cause, her social reputation, and her financial stability, she did not give up on life and stop trying. Neither did she become jealous of those around her who still had family, wealth, and respect, or embittered against a world that had imprisoned her husband, crushed her dreams of a good life, and imposed unreasonable restrictions on her just because she was a woman. Rather, she sat down to literally count her blessings—found not only in her own life but also in the lives of those around her, to whom she was connected in her very existence—and then gifted this treatise, the best of herself, to her daughter and the church.

Distinctively Female

I hope that by now, you have seen just how astounding it is that the only piece of systematic theology we have written by a woman in the seventeenth century is, rather than being "profoundly unfeminine," the exact opposite—"distinctively female," being produced and passed down generationally by the women of the family, from Hutchinson's mother, to Hutchinson, to Barbara.[38] In fact, Barbara would also have her own daughters and continue this chain. Unfortunately, we do not know what eventually became of Barbara; one source records that her daughters were "in the utmost distress and want" later in their lives, perhaps on a perpetual decline since Hutchinson's earlier losses.[39] But we can say that, despite this lack of worldly success, Hutchinson did her best to set up her daughter and her granddaughters for religious stability by not only teaching Barbara orally but also recording the fruits of her personal study in order to inspire them all to keep the faith and stick close to the church. Instead of closing herself off from the world, Hutchinson modeled a life that was intellectually active and promoted drawing close to other Christians and seeking peace and affinity with unbelievers where it could be rightly found. She showed Barbara that just because their family had suffered did not mean she had nothing to look forward to in the life ahead of her. Barbara had many good things coming her way—years of enjoying diverse seasons, elements, creatures, people, and books—and Hutchinson would say you do too, even if things seem dim. So I encourage you to borrow a page from Hutchinson's story and not give up when it is proving difficult to learn and teach or become hateful when it feels like the world is against you, but take the initiative to fulfill God's call of spiritual parenting on your life and maintain love for all believers, no matter their tradition, and even all of humankind, with whom you share the many blessings of life on this earth.

3

Mary Rich, Countess of Warwick

Wife as Philanthropist, Using Meditation

WITH ALL OF GOD'S great gifts to enjoy and share on this earth, we can sometimes slip into loving the stuff more than loving the people and the people more than God. This story is one of such upside-down affections turned right side up. Once upon a time, there was a wife who had a taste for the finer things in life and couldn't stop shopping, and a husband who had a bad temper and couldn't stop swearing. Sound familiar? I'm sure this could be a great many couples today, even if the roles were reversed. A love of stuff and lack of self-control are not uncommon. But, in some ways, this story is.

You see, six years into Mary's (1624–1678) longed-for marriage to Charles Rich, she had a conversion experience that took her off her path of worldliness and set her in a new way of intense devotion to God and generosity to others. Yet, Charles did not want to join her and, now chronically ill, was prone to picking fights. What was supposed to be a love match soon turned sour. I won't lie to you: the story of her marriage is a sad one. But Mary herself is not one to be pitied—in contrast to Charles's unbridled railings, she set out to control her own life, making it one of dignity and honor. By harnessing the deep desire in her heart for romance and fashion and redirecting it to God—the source of all true love and beauty—she brought substantial blessings into the lives of those who needed it most. But becoming this saintly, great-hearted force of a woman took a long time, and to appreciate her blossoming, we have to start at the beginning when she was just a bud.

Rich the Romantic

When Mary first met Charles, she was not a Christian; but she was a romance-lover! Growing up on novels and plays, she became preoccupied with a special kind of love.[1] Her autobiography shows us just this. In it, she recounts major turning points in her life, and after giving a brief account of her childhood, she begins the real story—the love story.

It went like this. When it was time for Mary to start considering marriage, her father attempted to set her up, multiple times, with firstborn sons (that is, those who would inherit their fathers' estates). She was not attracted to them, so it was easy for her to turn them down, being the romantic that she was. Apparently, Mary had no problem expressing her true feelings in full, as she wrote of one suitor, "My aversion for him was extraordinary."[2]

However, her refusal was not without consequences as it led her father to cut her off financially, and she soon ran into debt from her spending addiction. Although it was not socially acceptable in the seventeenth century for parents to force their children into marriage since there was to be some degree of "mutual sympathy," there was still an unsaid rule—in society and especially in Mary's household—that daughters must submit to arranged marriages.[3] Sadly, Mary's sisters suffered in their father's chosen matches (with three complaining of being mistreated by their husbands, another having to deal with an alcoholic, and the last being deserted), which may have also put Mary's mind to avoiding the same fate. Some of her sisters had even separated from their husbands, and though their father helped them during this difficult time, it seems that, beneath it all, he was mostly concerned about preserving the social connections that had originally drawn him to settle these unions in the first place. Though Mary and her sisters were raised with a façade of religion, their father's Protestantism was really just "a compound of chauvinism, egotism, and superstition," all bowing down to the gods of prestige and money.[4]

Thus, to her father's chagrin, the man that eventually caught Mary's attention was a younger brother. As a friend of her sister-in-law, Charles had spent some time with Mary and had, without words, expressed his affection for her. Over time, she recalled, "He did insensibly steal away my heart."[5] Yet, she knew her father would not approve and thus determined to end their more-than-friendship. However, every time she went to do it, she found herself unable to, and, she explained, "Thus we lived for some considerable time, my duty and my reason having frequent combats within me . . . [though] my passion . . . at last was always victorious."[6]

What would snap them out of this limbo was a case of measles. As Mary suffered from this illness, she was frequently visited by Charles. He faithfully attended to her, and, being warned by another family member that Mary's father would put an end to their relationship, he got down on both knees beside her sickbed to propose.

She said yes! But Charles's intel was right. The next day, knowing she had recovered enough to travel, Mary's father sent her away to the countryside, followed by two of her brothers sent to convince her to break off her engagement with Charles. In response to their efforts, she agreed to not marry without her father's consent—but she would marry no one except Charles. Though his fortune was smaller and she was used to living with more, he was a good person who came from a good family, and she could be content with that because she loved him. Seeing that she wouldn't be persuaded otherwise and having a respect for Charles's father, Mary's father eventually gave his consent, though he decreased her dowry. Mary and Charles wed privately and were off to live with his parents at their properties in Leighs and London.

Sadly, Mary would end up regretting this disobedience to her father for many years to come, but marrying into Charles's family did prove to give her a significant blessing that would change the course of her life—true religion. Mary's father- and mother-in-law not only encouraged Christian living but also practiced it themselves, and their kind dispositions and good hearts captivated her own. She became close with them, and their love for godliness rubbed off on her. Later, she would describe her father-in-law as a "worthy" man who, in the seventeen years she lived with him, was "the most civil, kind, and obliging father that ever any person had."[7] It seemed that now, compared to the fake faith she was raised with, Mary had found something real. Yet, she admitted that in her early days with Charles's family, she only wanted to please them, rather than God himself. She had felt the appeal of Christianity but had not actually repented.

However, all of that would change when Rich became a mother. Tragically, her daughter Elizabeth died in infancy, so when her second-born—a son named Charles—fell ill, she desperately pleaded with God to save him and promised that she would change. Though God had by this point awakened her to the state of her soul and she had promised to repent, temptations—usually brought on by being around her old friends and old lifestyle—kept her from fulfilling such promises. Thus, when young Charles was healed, Rich instinctively had the urge to go into the quiet of Leighs, something she had never liked to do before. It was during her time in the countryside, in search of Spirit and solitude, that she was finally able to commit herself to God. One of the main factors that helped her along to real repentance was an Anglican chaplain named Anthony Walker. His preaching enabled her to interpret her past, helping her realize that when she married, she only cared about nice clothes and doing fun things and was "steadfastly set against being a Puritan."[8] It also helped her start a new future. Though she had a history of being flaky, this decision stuck, and she now began to develop what would become an intense, lifelong practice of devotion to God.[9] Soon, her friends noticed a change in her life, and when she had a serious case of smallpox and feared she might die, she had come to trust God so fully that she knew whatever happened would be his will.

Yet, it was not Mary who would suddenly die but Charles's brother and father. Thus, years after all the drama about Mary's love life, the younger brother she married came to unexpectedly inherit the family estate. Charles and Mary also took custody of their three nieces: Ann, Mary, and Essex. Of course, Mary was heartbroken to lose her beloved father-in-law—but she was also nervous about falling back into her old spendthrift ways. However, now that she had experienced a true conversion, she actually did the opposite by wisely managing the household—caring personally for servants, visitors, and the three girls—and by increasing her charitable giving to pastors, students, and those in need such as widows and refugees.

This was no hobby for Rich; it required serious work on her part. Becoming a countess meant she "could now formalize her charities and permit the poor to petition her in her own home" as well as welcome the poor at an "open still-house, where they could receive medicines and care."[10] She also oversaw the estate's accounts and the many clergy livings and was always bringing someone into her home or going out to offer relief, including on Christmas Eve, which was a time of "lavish charity to the poor."[11] Overall, she was the perfect example of what Sara Mendelson calls the seventeenth-century "female elite" who, though we think of them as "a leisure class," were actually "hard-working supervisors of large and complex households" as well as "capable administrators of medical and charitable institutions."[12]

For the Riches, two deaths in a row must have felt like enough. But that is not often how life goes, and soon another tragedy struck. Shortly after getting married and moving in with them, their son Charles came down with the same dreaded smallpox that had once almost taken Rich's life. Having already experienced the illness herself and feeling especially protective of her only child, who had been close to death once before, she quickly took control by sending everyone out of the house to prevent the spread of disease and caring for him alone. Though the doctors said he would recover, he soon died. Rich's husband broke down when he heard the news and fell into a depression for some time, and Rich found little physical or emotional comfort in the following days other than the use of Epsom waters, the company of Chaplain Walker and her cherished sister Katherine, and the confidence she had that her son was with God.[13] Rich recalled, "I confess that I loved [my son] at a rate . . . [that] I could, with all the willingness in the world, have died either for him or with him, if God had only seen it fit."[14] From that point on, she never entered that house again and asked her husband to sell it.

Later in life, as she thought of her son often and even held days of remembrance for him, Rich would not only recognize the deep, "inexpressible grief" of losing her "only son," but also the broad, far-reaching grief of not having any more children and thus being able to write such empty words as, "I am childless."[15] She had understandably come to regret her and her husband's initial desire to not have more children after Elizabeth and Charles in order to preserve Mary's physique and the inheritance they hoped to pass on.

Sadly, as such events were taking place, another evil began to sneak through the door, one that was slow and cumulative. For about ten years Rich's husband had been suffering from gout (as well as other illnesses) and, for the next ten, would continue to greatly deteriorate. Toward the end of his life, Rich witnessed an "almost daily dying" during which Charles eventually "lost the use of his limbs, and never put his feet to the ground, nor was able to feed himself, nor turn in his bed but by the help of his servants, and by those constant pains he was so weakened and wasted that he was like a mere skeleton."[16] The man she once described as "very cheerful, and handsome, well-bred, and fashioned . . . and being good company" now became a shadow of his former self in every way.[17] In the diary she kept, Rich would recount time after time of him picking fights with her for no reason, her continual caring for him by his bedside (reading books and attending to his needs), and only a few occasions when he could come down for dinner or leave the house with her. Rich's relentless devotion to God as well as her ongoing attempts to discuss eternity and censure his profanity seemed to bother him, so much so that he once even prevented her from going to church, though he sometimes listened to her with an open mind.

We may wonder why Rich put up with such disrespectful, even abusive, behavior for so long instead of following in her sisters' paths of separation. But that was the decision she made. Perhaps she could not let go of the man she had fallen in love with even though he had changed so much or she sympathized with his bodily state and couldn't bear to let him die alone. Perhaps she had too firm a commitment to the institution of marriage to give up, was scared of losing her financial stability, or was holding out hope that he would one day change for the better. Maybe, it was a little bit of each. Regardless, she herself said that when her husband eventually succumbed to his illness, it was only then that she entered, in her words, "the greatest trial of my life."[18] She solemnly recalled,

> I was more afflicted than ever before for anything in my fore-
> past life; for though my son's death had almost sunk me, and
> my grief for him was so great that I thought it almost impos-
> sible to be more sensibly afflicted, yet I found now I was so,

and though God had given me many years to provide for our separation . . . yet I still flattered myself with hopes of his life.[19]

At this time she was so depressed that she began fantasizing about her own death. In fact, Raymond A. Anselment explains that Rich's "account of her physical and spiritual state" during and after her husband's death "is unusual among women's diaries and memoirs [of the seventeenth century] in the considerable emphasis on her despondency."[20] She recalls that the only thing that helped was telling herself that she had done everything in her power to aid him physically and spiritually and would now do her best to follow the instructions in his "exasperatingly complicated" will, as he had made her the only executor and handed over his entire estate for her to manage.[21]

Thus began Rich's final years of stewarding her financial and relational inheritance. She continued to actively give to charity and only grew in her reputation as "a revered leader in her local Essex community, settling disputes between neighbours, arranging an equitable distribution of income to ministers of various denominations, and giving away a third or more of her income to the poor, the clergy, and local institutions such as Felsted School."[22] She also continued to guide her nieces, who had become like daughters to her. Rich took care of them when they were ill, offered advice, celebrated their eventual marriages, visited them when they gave birth to their own children, and consoled them when they experienced loss. For example, she supported Essex's decision to turn down a suitor—though Rich had personally wanted Essex to marry him—because it was her free choice. And after young Mary lost her firstborn child, Rich took her to Richard

Baxter, a Puritan minister famous for his wise pastoral counseling who Rich had befriended.[23]

At the end of her autobiography, Rich praised God for helping her execute her husband's will to every family member's satisfaction, without disputes. Though she had married into the Riches as a hopeless romantic and unrepentant, materialistic girl who grew up surrounded by false religion, she would become the one to preserve both their estate and their godly reputation, harnessing such resources for the good of the entire community. Not surprisingly, she kept these up even after her death via stipulations in her own will to provide for her servants and continue her charity work for several months, as well as bestow gifts on those ministers and family members who had been especially precious to her.

Bending the Mind

Though the bountifulness of Rich's charitable giving may be the most outwardly impressive aspect of her life, it seems that what enabled her to live so open-handedly before others was the fact that she had lived open-heartedly before God. When I said that Rich practiced intense devotion, I was not exaggerating; she herself described it as "my tedious rules" for holy living.[24] Every day, she would rise early to meditate for two hours in a wooded area outside her house, which she called "the wilderness." The regularity with which she visited the same place at the same time to do the same thing seemed to facilitate familiarity with God. She once wrote in her diary that when going into the wilderness,

> I no sooner come into the walks, which I used to meditate in, but God stirred up in me spiritual breathings and pantings after

him: when I was there I had a particular reason to remember; for once when I was so troubled that I thought I should sink under my burden and never be able to take it up more, God was pleased there so to comfort me, and assure me of being happy in his favor, that I went away cheerful and composed.[25]

These woods—where she had "seen the first sprouting, growth, and flourishing . . . and almost daily taken delight in"—became infused with meaning, history, and relationship; it was the place she always met with God, so when she went there, he was always there to greet her.[26]

After these meditations, Rich would return to her room to read Scripture and pray, and before bed each night she would recall her sins, confess them to God, and ask for forgiveness. On Sundays, in addition to this regime, she would attend two sermons as well as catechize her household, which involved reading and listening to her nieces and servants. And, of course, during the week she would spend much time doling out funds, hosting ministers, and caring for friends and family.

Yet, none of this was meant to be practiced rotely. In fact, such shallow, even fake worship was the exact thing that Puritans like Mary Rich openly denounced, as they felt it was a common problem in their society. Thus, when Rich spent time in spiritual disciplines, she attempted to fully apply herself to communing with God: not to the practices themselves but to God himself. This emphasis on sincere communion meant that her devotions did not always go as planned. Sometimes she found "divine gusto," but other times her mind wandered and her heart was "dull," "backward," and "discomposed"; she recalled being oppressed by hot weather and forced to move inside, being interrupted by visitors, and having her schedule overrun with chores.[27] After something stressful happened—like an argument with her husband or the time her brother got so sick she thought he was going to die—Rich felt unable to do any devotions at all. It seems she even had a lengthy pause in her wilderness meditations during the months surrounding her husband's final days and death, probably feeling lost in grief.[28] Overall, what was important was not being perfect but making a real effort each day to be with God—truly focusing on and spending time with him on a regular basis and knowing he was never far away when life was falling apart and the best laid plans had to be tossed out the window.

Not surprisingly, Rich often referred to God as her best friend—like her other friends, but even better, since he would always be there for her and never got sick of her. For example, after a sorrowful parting with her sister Katherine, who she was very close to, Rich wrote in her diary, "Yet my best Friend stayed with me."[29] Similarly, in a meditation, she once reflected on the fact that her friends might sometimes tire of seeing her, but God never did, writing, "My dearest friends . . . love me ever so well, yet my company may sometimes be unseasonable to them, and therefore for the present [they] would be glad to be rid of me. Yet in my longest and frequentest approaches to [God's] divine majesty I never found that any hour rendered them unseasonable."[30]

Thus, being with God was the purpose of meditation, which was defined in the seventeenth century as the "bending of the mind" upon an object or topic in order to draw spiritual meaning out of it to use for devotion.[31] Theologians of the time distinguished between two types of meditation—*occasional* (which was brief and informal, spontaneously inspired by observing the outward world) and *deliberate* (which was lengthier and more formal, coming out of a time of focused contemplation on a biblical passage or theological doctrine). Rich herself seemed to know of these distinctions, as she recorded meditations of her own and also provided a wonderful description of and instructions for how to use deliberate meditation in a letter to her friend the Earl of Berkeley who had asked to hear her rules for holy living. When she addressed meditation in her response to Berkeley (who was just one of several people she inspired to use this practice), she first debunked a common misunderstanding. You and I might be prone to think of meditation as a lonely affair, but Rich sets us straight. She poetically reasoned that "the way not to be alone is to be alone, and you will find yourself never less alone than when you are so. For certainly the God that makes all others good company, must needs be best himself."[32]

Then, Rich offered Berkeley some ideas for what to meditate on, instructing him to first attend his mind to the temporality of earthly things and the end of his life. She advised:

> I would, therefore, have you meditate sometimes on the tran-
> sitoriness and dissatisfyingness of all this world's glories. Your
> lordship yourself has, as young as you are, seen such strange
> revolutions, as are sufficient to convince you, that there is noth-
> ing certain in this life. . . . Next I would have you meditate
> sometimes upon the shortness of your life, and the uncertainty
> of the time of your death . . . and on the great account you
> must give of all you have done in the flesh.[33]

Yet, Berkeley must not sit on these thoughts forever, as they could be depressing; he must press on to happy thoughts of heaven. Rich explained:

> I would not keep you upon such melancholy thoughts as these too long, and therefore I would have you think of the joys of heaven; of that rest which remains for the people of God; of that better country; . . . and of those joys which eye has not seen, nor ear heard, nor has it ever entered into the heart of man to conceive what God has laid up for them that love him. . . . We shall be past . . . suffering, ill. There all the tears shall be wiped from our eyes . . . Such meditations as these I would have you frequent in, that while you are musing the fire of heavenly devotion may burn and inflame your heart with love to God, so that your meditation of him may be sweet.[34]

Thus, when Rich described the emotional effects of religion in her letter, she said that it was not something that makes people sad but something that gives them peace and ultimately enables them to lead a cheerful existence, which is enjoyable not just for them but also for those whose paths they cross in all areas of life.

In addition to these instructions for Berkeley, Rich also kept a record of her own meditations, which reveal her knack for observation. A spinning spider made her think of works-righteousness, countless stars in the sky were God's amazing promises, sealing a letter with hot wax reminded her of following through on resolutions, and a mother lifting a child up a step was like God carrying her soul over spiritual stumbling blocks. These illustrations may sound simple, but they reveal her keen eye for movement and meaning and draw the reader in with their "personal immediacy."[35] In fact, they were the most thoroughly developed occasional meditations written by a woman in the seventeenth century and the only ones to be published.[36] The chaplain who printed them, Rich's friend and mentor Walker, said in her funeral sermon that this practice was her crowning glory. He stated,

> if she exceeded herself in anything as much as she excelled others in most things, it was in meditation: this was her masterpiece . . . both in set times and occasional. In the first, choosing some select subject, which she would press upon her heart with intensest thoughts till she had drawn out all its juice and nourishment; and in the second, like a spiritual bee, she would suck honey from all occurrences, whole volumes of which she has left behind her.[37]

Walker did not exaggerate—Rich's meditations were varied and voluminous. She noticed animals like horses, sea anemones, snails, and her dogs as well as human activities like ballet, breast-feeding, bloodletting, and bullying. She wrote about inanimate objects like boats, sundials, telescopes, mouse traps, mines, and maps as well as consumables like tea, apples, peaches, and honey-comb. And she took note of natural phenomena, like sunsets and fires, relating all of these regular life things to spiritual themes like temptation, hypocrisy, thankfulness, and original sin. There are so many we could now look at, but in the spirit of focusing our minds like Rich did, let's take a deep dive into just a few that address two important themes in her faith story—anger and charity.

A Sweet River and Sudden Tempest

It is the sad truth that anger was a regular part of Rich's life. In her diary she recalled that sometimes, though she had determined to not engage her husband when he became angry, his poor treatment affected her so deeply that she would give in to arguing with him, even though she only said true and right things, and would once in a while mutter frustrations under her breath as she stormed out of the room or end up getting in another spat with her nieces. Such fights with Charles greatly troubled her, so much so that she once told him, "I [am] weary of my life" and would sometimes feel physically ill after an argument.[38] Yet, what we will see in her meditations on anger is that Rich wasn't just passively reacting to the actions of others—she was taking control of her own actions, her own relationship with God, and making her life what she wanted it to be, no matter what Charles or anyone else did. There was an ugly side to Rich's marriage, but she turned the ugliness on its head to make her own beauty, in her own soul, and with the hopes of spreading it to others.

Overall, one of her best meditations on anger was prompted by looking out a window of her London residence at the Thames River. As she stared at this scene, she noticed how stark the contrast was between the river's serene flow and the aggressive waves it could produce. Rich observed that

> this sweet river . . . that I looked upon with so much pleasure and delighted to do so for a long time together while it was smooth . . . yet afterwards when a sudden and violent tempest

storm arose, what was before so alluring to me to view while it was serene and calm, did afterwards when the waves were rough prove rather frightful to me than delightful and made me shut my window to keep me from longer seeing it.[39]

This change made her more clearly see how anger could alter a person's countenance and how this affects the feelings of those around them. She realized that someone who is calm is "alluring and attractive," having beautiful body language and a beautiful face, but, if they suddenly become angry, their appearance changes so much that it turns people off from them.[40]

Rich did not want to ever look like this. So she cried out,

O Lord, I most humbly beseech you, by this meditation make me more than ever . . . to practice those Christian adorning graces of meekness and patience by which I shall evince to others . . . the great beauty there is in being calm and being freed from unbeseeming and violent passions, that I may not force my beholders so to dislike me as to be dissatisfied with coming near me but may by sweetness and gentleness adorn my holy profession and excite others to be imitators of those graces.[41]

Thus, though Rich was no doubt reminded of her husband's anger, she did not focus on him but on her own, positive actions, affirming to herself that beauty—the quality she had been so interested in since she was young—was found in a calm demeanor. Not only this, but freedom and friendship were also gained with serenity. Rich knew that while anger might seem like a way to take control, it is actually something that enslaves and alienates, and she knew that she didn't want that for her life and, most importantly, that God didn't either.

Reflecting on Jonah 4:9 helped her to further think about how anger can affect a person's relationship with God. Here, Jonah was so upset at God for being merciful to the Ninevites that he not only failed to confess this as a sin but "seemed to dare to approve it even to [God's] very face."[42] This showed Rich the irrationality of anger, in that it can make someone lose their reason so fully that they "are ready to justify a fault instead of begging pardon for it."[43] Just as she was disturbed by the raging river, so does she find Jonah's attitude to be repulsive, and thus asked God to help her not act like him. She prayed,

> O Lord, I do therefore most humbly beseech you to enable me to be slow to anger, remembering that you have told me that he that is slow to anger is better than the mighty, and he that governs his spirit than he that takes a city; and he that has no rule over his spirit is as a city that has no wall. Oh bring all my passions into subjection to my reason, and my reason to my religion. Let me not fret myself in any ways to do evil, nor to be angry, and sin in my anger; but give me a meek, quiet, contented spirit, which is in your sight of great value.[44]

Rich knew she was a victim of her husband's anger rather than the perpetrator, writing in her diary phrases like "I was in no fault" regarding their fights.[45] Yet, she still admitted that it was a challenge to not reply to anger with anger and asked God to help her keep her cool rather than respond in a reactionary way, recognizing that anger was not just ugly, enslaving, and alienating but even delusive. And, just as she affirmed to herself that being calm brought beauty, freedom, and friendship, so did she here motivate herself to be calm by affirming that if she did so, she would be better than someone trying to wield power. All in all, Rich felt sorrow and regret over her marriage, but she didn't wallow in self-pity. In fact, she used this exact point of pain in her life to do something amazing—run an influential charitable organization built on her husband's inheritance.

The Dam That Stops the Current of Charity

As mentioned earlier, Rich's great generosity did not develop in a vacuum but was prompted by her use of meditation. In fact, it was inherently linked to the nature of such meditations, as they made her contemplate her relationship with the very physical objects she observed. These simultaneously led her to be thankful for all she had in life and to see the vanity of using material things for self-satisfaction as contrasted with their usefulness for helping those in need. Rich's many diary entries confirm this, as she often found herself being led from looking at creation around her, to thanking God, to being inspired to share such blessings with others. She recognized that she came to, in her words, "sweet Leighs . . . the gift of God" in order "to possess houses full of all good things I filled not, gardens and orchards which I planted not," and repeatedly said things like "at my table I was affected to consider the plenty God was there pleased to give me; and my heart was carried out to pity those who wanted those mercies I enjoyed."[46] Rich was someone who was not only aware of the things around her but also of the people around her and was able to effectively calculate the worth of each one.

In addition to spurring on her charity, Rich's meditations also positively affected how she gave and how she viewed the people who she gave to. For example, in one meditation about a patch of dry ground with a big crack next to a patch with no cracks, Rich was reminded that underprivileged people come from different backgrounds and thus may seek help in different ways. She reasoned,

> Some who have had an ingenuous and plentiful education and afterwards are by God's providence reduced to want are many times content rather to conflict with great necessities than by opening their mouths to beg [and] declare their sad condition, whereas others who want the modesty which the other's breeding has given them no sooner have any manner of want of former plenty but presently seek relief by proclaiming with open mouth their necessities to be great and insupportable, though indeed much less than the others who conceal them.[47]

Thus, Rich prayed that God would help her when dispensing charity to not think that she was "bound to give most to them that ask most" but rather could choose to give to those most in need by investigating who that was, even if they didn't speak up the loudest.[48] Similarly, when Rich was approached by a woman who did not look ill but had a serious condition and was desperate for medication, Rich was led to help her after listening to her story.

In another meditation, Rich used a sheep, munching away on some grass, to remind herself that wealth was not an indicator of godliness. Just as God enables the sheep to eat "so close to the ground" where there seems to be no grass, though there is enough to survive, so does God provide for his people, even if his provision seems small.[49] This made Rich pray that God would help her to not respect wealthy people more than poor people, as the prosperous are not always good and those "poor in the world" can be "rich in faith."[50] Thus, by taking into account the fact that those in need are unique individuals who are not less valuable than the wealthy, Rich elevated her charity from a pretentious, tightfisted, unintentional, detached, and indistinguishing flow of funds to a thoughtful, personal, and open-handed act that humbly dignified the recipient.

Yet, her most elegant meditations on charity center on a dam and a silkworm. The goodness of giving to others was once reaffirmed to Rich when she saw a dam that was stopping water and realized it was like a wealthy person who had been given so much by God yet hoarded it, cutting it off from those it was intended to be shared with. She noted that just as the dam was put up by a man in order to keep all the water to himself, so do rich people sometimes keep their wealth for themselves even though God gave it to them for the very purpose of having them give it to others. The expensive clothing and furniture they buy to adorn their bodies and homes create "the dam which stops the current of their charity, and keeps it back from the poor and indigent, whose wants would be comfortably supplied by their superfluities."[51]

This observation led Rich not to rail against others, though she could have easily done so, for she had many connections with court life (being "on familiar terms with Queen Katherine") and considered high society to be a hindrance to devotion rather than something to be admired and attained.[52] But instead, knowing that she was tempted to only spend on herself, she prayed that God would remind her of her past guiltiness in this area and consider that he had made her a vessel of his alms so that she wouldn't dam up what should be given liberally to refresh others. She continued,

> O let me willingly starve a lust to feed a saint. And let me remember that he that sows sparingly, shall reap sparingly. And let me not only now and then drop a little for charity; but make me one of those persons mentioned in your word, who by being liberal, devise liberal things, and by so doing are established. Oh, make me, as it were, an open floodgate to water my neighbors' necessities. . . . Oh make me to do so as far as I am able, but especially make me remember the household of faith.[53]

Now do you see why I said her great devotion to God led to her great charity?

Rich becomes even more specific in a meditation on a silkworm, wherein she considered the origin, use, and destiny of expensive clothing. Upon noticing this creepy crawler, she noted:

> This may be useful to caution me against loving and delighting in fine silks when I do consider that all the finest and best mingled ones that can be put to adorn me with are all spun by a poor worm and that to be proud of fine clothes is to be so of that which is the monument of our sin, for if Adam had not sinned, we should have had no need of clothing to have hid our shame.[54]

Rich hits the nail on the head with this insight into Scripture, creation, and human nature. What irony, what stupidity, to think the thing we need to cover up our disgrace could be used to make us impressive!

She continues on, noting that this is the reality of all fine things, including pearls, crimson dye, and precious metals like gold and silver. Yet, Rich is not unreasonable or blind to the realities of earthly living. In fact, they were ever before her face as the manager of a wealthy household, full of "valuable consumer goods [that had to] be maintained and cared for, such as fine linens and delicate lace."[55] So it is not surprising to find in her meditation that she includes a short aside about Proverbs 31, explaining why nice things in themselves are not sinful. She posits that because the virtuous woman clothes her household in fine materials, this means that it must not be wrong to wear nice clothes and that "the silkworm was not made only to spin for the proud."[56]

Thus, Rich's denunciation of the high life and commitment to charitable giving was not motivated by some form of extreme asceticism—unnecessarily denying oneself good gifts from God or devaluing the bodily, material, and physical, as if there were something inherently evil about them. Rather, she recognized the goodness of the silkworm and its ability to create a substance that can be made into clothing, which fills a basic human need for warmth, protection, and modesty and can be enjoyed. What is sinful is focusing only on the material instead of the immaterial and on only indulging our own desires instead of filling the needs of others. So, getting back to her own life, Rich laments that she loved nice clothes too much and her soul too little, and prays that God would help her not yield to the temptation of "esteem[ing] either others or [her]self upon the account of being set out with much bravery."[57]

However, she does not stop here. In Rich's mind, killing vanity in her heart is only the beginning; she must then become heavenly minded and generous. Thus, she asks God, "Let me value more others—my fellow Christians—and prize more in myself the adorning of a sweet, meek, quiet, contented spirit . . . And if it be adorned with the graces of thy Holy Spirit, help me to consider they will make me fine to all eternity."[58]

Rich also knows from her past experience that resolutions might fall through if you don't make a plan and find ways to motivate yourself to stick to it, so she asks God to help her remember times that she chose generosity over greed and how it made her feel so that, in the heat of the moment, she can make the right choice. She asks:

Make me often call to my remembrance the very great and sensible pleasure I have often experienced in clothing naked backs, when you have let me have the honor of being your almoner and disperse your charity through my hands to your necessitous poor. And let that make me rather to choose to clothe naked backs than to please idle eyes and rather to choose to see many of my fellow creatures kept warm, being covered with my charity in plain but warm apparel, than to starve my charity by putting upon myself one rich, laced gown which would, if sold and distributed unto the poor, make many decent and convenient gowns for several indigent persons.[59]

This is the perfect example of why such meditation on things in the natural world was so helpful to Rich. It not only taught her to stop, acknowledge, and make the most of the regular happenings in her daily life but also set before her eyes a concrete, indisputable image of what she was hoping would shape her heart.

The Ripple Effects of Meditation

At first glance, it might be tempting to write Rich off as a holier-than-thou type, someone who liked to obsess over rules and rub her perfection in everyone else's faces. But only a slightly harder look shows us that this was not at all the case. For one thing, she knew her shortcomings—the many times she attempted to meditate, pray, or read Scripture, but failed—and asked God to cover them in grace. She also used her meditations to draw out the sin stuck in her heart and had a time of confession every night. And, perhaps most importantly, she hoped and prayed and worked so that her devotion to God would be uplifting for others, not condemning. The times she reproved her husband, donated money to underprivileged folk, and instructed those in her care, she had their well-being in mind—not her own goodness, but promoting their good. While we may want to accuse Rich of being overbearing, we should remember that one reason she wanted others to spend time with God was so that they would experience the immense happiness it would bring to their souls, so much more than any worldly things could.

In fact, this devotion and service all flowed from God himself, who must be the first aim of all our exercises. It was his transformative friendship that enabled Rich to keep noticing blessings and connecting with people even when her life did not pan out the way she hoped it would. Rich never did lose her sentimental heart, keen on finding true love; she simply discovered its fulfillment in God. And though she may have later lost the romance she had found as a young woman, she gave her community a wonderfully grand gesture of love, positively affecting the lives of so many and setting her name down in history as a great female philanthropist, a great lover of humankind.

So, in learning from Rich, the last thing we want to become is a self-flogging ascetic or a self-righteous nag. To avoid these, we must spend time before the face of God, baring our souls and sins, thanking him for his good gifts, and asking for his forgiveness. What Rich teaches us is that when we sincerely and intentionally apply our whole selves in times of devotion, we will be led to a true spirituality, one that makes room for a daily repenting of our own sin, finds a reason for gratitude around every bush and creek, enjoys intimacy with God, and loves others instead of despising, coddling, or looking down on them. And when we spend regular quality time with God, not only to love him and get his love for ourselves but also to then give his love to others—regardless of what they chose to do with their lives and whether or not they are worthy—we imitate God himself, as he gives out of his abundance not because of another's goodness but because he is good. Walker rightly reminds us that though the people Rich gave herself to were sometimes undeserving, this did not discourage her from giving again, "for though they deceived her in giving, God would not deceive her in accepting what was sincerely done for his name's sake."[60]

4

Anne Bradstreet

Grandmother as Homemaker, Using Prayer

JUST AS THE LORD'S PRESENCE can turn loneliness to love, so can it turn a foreign land into a home. The life of the most famous American female Puritan shows just such a transformation. Have you ever gone to a new place, maybe a party at someone's house you've never been to or a country you've never visited, and felt like a total outsider? As someone who thrives with routine and is slow to emotionally adapt to change—unfamiliar sights, smells, sounds, and unknowns—I feel that way with all first experiences, even small ones. So I can hardly imagine making a permanent trip across the ocean from one continent to another (not planning on returning!) and having to call it my home.

Yet, this is exactly what newlywed Anne Bradstreet (c. 1612–1672) had to do at the age of eighteen. When she disembarked the *Arbella* and set foot in New England with her husband and parents, she was shocked. It did not feel right at all; how was she ever going to live there, never mind set up house and start a family?

Bradstreet the Immigrant

The reason that Anne's family had set off on this risky voyage in the first place was because they had concluded—like many other Puritans at the time—that the best way to live out their religious convictions was to leave England and its persecution. Yet, though her parents were wealthy enough to make their ocean crossing as painless as was possible at the time, their arrival in Salem, Massachusetts, marked the beginning of a long, hard transition. As Anne's father noted in a letter back to their home country, "We found the colony in a sad and unexpected condition, above eight of them being dead the winter before, and many of those alive weak and sick, all the corn and bread amongst them all hardly sufficient to feed them a fortnight."[1] This did not improve even a year later as he recorded in another letter, written hunched over on the floor as they still had no table, that

> there is not a house where is not one dead, and some houses many . . . the natural causes seem to be in the want of warm lodging and good diet, to which Englishmen are habituated at home, and the sudden increase of heat which they endure who are landed here in summer . . . for those only these two last years died of fevers who landed in June or July, as those of Plymouth, who landed in the winter, died of the scurvy.[2]

No doubt such physical conditions would have disturbed Anne, but it seems she also felt ill at ease about the change in culture, as she would later recall, "I found a new world and new manners, at which my heart rose. But after I was convinced it was the way of God, I submitted to it and joined to the church at Boston."[3]

Crafting Poems

A few years later, Bradstreet would give birth to Samuel (and then Dorothy, Sarah, Simon, Hannah, Mercy, Dudley, and John) after praying to get pregnant for what she said felt like forever. Soon she had to manage a growing household. But, with the help of servants, she was also able to spend time on one of her greatest passions—crafting her own poetry. Her subjects ranged from literature (like the famous Renaissance poets she had studied as a girl), to politics (like the reign of Queen Elizabeth and the Civil War in England), to the Bible and theology (like David and Jonathan's story and the vanity of life on earth). Similar to other writers of the time, Bradstreet shared these poems with her family and friends, and at one point, her brother-in-law decided to take them with him to England to be printed there. This fateful act set Bradstreet's name down in history as the first person in America— female or male—to publish a book of poetry. However, according to Bradstreet, she did not know they were getting published and thus began making corrections to what had been printed as well as writing new poems about her parents, the natural world, and the conflict between the flesh and the spirit.

In addition to these published pieces, Bradstreet also wrote prayer-poems about her family life, recording her feelings about giving birth, the return of her son after a trip to England, the intimate love she shared with her husband, receiving letters from him when he was away, deliverance from her many illnesses, the fire that destroyed their home, and the deaths of her daughter-in-law and several grand-children. It is clear from these family poems that Bradstreet was the type of person who felt triumphs and tragedies in life very acutely. As she said in a letter to her children, "I have often been perplexed that I have not found that constant joy in my pilgrimage" and though having experienced "tastes of sweetness . . . yet have I many times sinkings and droopings, and not enjoyed that felicity that sometimes I have done."[4] The way she dealt with these emotional ups and downs—especially the downs—was by reminding herself to go to God. She continued, "But when I have been in darkness and seen no light, yet have I desired to stay myself upon the Lord."[5] And sometimes, it seems, this was done through writing poetry.

Yet, when Bradstreet was penning such praises and laments to God about her life, she was not only writing them to express her own emotions—they were also meant for her family. By doing this, she effectively implemented a kind of liturgy for their shared existence. Just as she had helped build a home from the ground up, starting with less than a table to write on, and plant a church, which started with less than one hundred adults, so did she set up a spiritual and emotional structure for her family to reorient themselves when they personally encountered dark times, thereby keeping them under God's care and keeping them together.

That Trunk, That Chest, Thy Table

Overall, one of the darkest time for the Bradstreet family was when their house burned down. Not only had they suffered the sacrifices and pains of first immigrating to New England and then having to move several times, as well as building an entire life for their growing family in this unfamiliar place, but they also had meaningful items from England as well as invaluable pieces of work in progress stored in their home.

Seeing the sudden and total destruction of possessions that had sentimental value for the Bradstreet family—like furniture, clothing, household tools, and family portraits—is difficult to watch; but perhaps even worse than this was the disintegration of Bradstreet's books, edits to her published poems, and copies of new poems.[6] Her son Simon would note in his diary that his family had lost their over eight-hundred-piece book collection, which was massive for that time and probably functioned as a kind of community library. Further, Bradstreet herself recalls, "My papers fell a prey to th' raging fire."[7] Thanks to the culture of manuscript circulation, she was probably able to "ask . . . relatives to return or transcribe poems that she had sent them," but it seems this did not work for all her poems, as she "abandoned working on" one of her very long pieces "when her drafts were destroyed."[8] Yet, in an act of sheer creativity, even pointed rebellion against the loss of paper and pen, Bradstreet set to writing down a kind of elegy for their family home in order to help them work through the emotional, material, financial, and vocational fallout of such an event.

As she opens her poem, she seems to instinctively know that to work through trauma, you have to express exactly what happened and how you felt. Thus, she starts at the startling beginning, recalling,

> In silent night when rest I took
> For sorrow near I did not look
> I wakened was with thund'ring noise
> And piteous shrieks of dreadful voice.

That fearful sound of "Fire!" and "Fire!"
Let no man know is my desire.[9]

Even in this exact moment of terror, with her own life and that
of her family members in danger, Bradstreet's heart flew up to
God. She wrote,

I, starting up, the light did spy,
And to my God my heart did cry
To strengthen me in my distress
And not to leave me succorless.[10]

Yet, once she properly sees the disaster happening before her,
she has to look away because it is too much for her heart to bear.
She continues,

Then, coming out, beheld a space
The flame consume my dwelling place.
And when I could no longer look,
I blest His name that gave and took,
That laid my goods now in the dust.
Yea, so it was, and so 'twas just.
It was His own, it was not mine,
Far be it that I should repine;
He might of all justly bereft
But yet sufficient for us left.[11]

Here, Bradstreet reminds herself of her theological beliefs about
God as the Creator and provider of all good things—he had given

them all of this stuff and this entire house, and so it ultimately belonged to him.

Yet, affirming God's right to give and take away did not mean that she couldn't also recognize the pain she and her family felt in this providence, and so she rightly paid tribute to their beautiful home. Such recognition is not a faithless, illegitimate questioning of God, but a rational, proper response to having to say goodbye to a good gift. Thus Bradstreet worked up the courage to walk through the wreckage, looking at what was once the place that her husband, children, and grandchildren hosted guests, ate, chatted, and told stories. As she walks, she speaks to the house "as if it were a family member who took part in the shared activities of everyday life."[12] She remembers,

When by the ruins oft I past
My sorrowing eyes aside did cast,
And here and there the places spy
Where oft I sat and long did lie:
Here stood that trunk, and there that chest,
There lay that store I counted best.
My pleasant things in ashes lie,
And them behold no more shall I.
Under thy roof no guest shall sit,
Nor at thy table eat a bit.
No pleasant tale shall e're be told,
Nor things recounted done of old.
No candle e'er shall shine in thee,
Nor bridegroom's voice e'er heard shall be.
In silence ever shall thou lie,
Adieu, Adieu, all's vanity.[13]

Here, Bradstreet becomes very specific by looking at "that" trunk and "that" chest.[14] These items were not just things. They made up the place where her family spent their days together, literally becoming a family.

For Bradstreet, the home was the center of family life; this is seen throughout her other poems, where she often refers to it as a nest. In a piece about raising her children, she reminisced,

> I had eight birds hatched in one nest,
> Four cocks there were, and hens the rest.
> I nursed them up with pain and care,
> Nor cost, nor labor did I spare.
> Till at last they felt their wing,
> Mounted the trees, and learned to sing;
> Chief of the brood then took his flight,
> To regions far and left me quite.
> My mournful chirps I after send,
> Till he return, or I do end:
> Leave not thy nest, thy dame and sire,
> Fly back and sing amidst this choir.[15]

This nest was where their lives began and where Bradstreet called them home, and they would eventually create nests for their own families, as her eldest, Samuel, had already.

Similarly, Bradstreet finds inherent value in earthly items as useful for our pilgrimage on earth and as signposts, pointing us to better things in heaven. For example, she described her father as someone who owned his possessions "as a pilgrim."[16] In a meditation on Jonah she compared his gourd to "all the comforts of this life," saying we naturally "take great delight for a season in them and find their shadow very comfortable," though they eventually get eaten by worms, thus reminding us that they were temporary and making us look to heaven.[17] We do not truly own anything and our physical comforts on earth are mere shadows of heavenly comfort, but there is a sense in which we have, use, and enjoy them precisely because they are given by God for the purpose of being used and enjoyed, thereby enriching our life here and giving us a taste of the even greater gifts to come.

Thus, though Bradstreet must speak to her heart to remind it that this earthly house was temporary, she also finds hope in the heavenly—and therefore ultimate—version of home, the eternal home that makes the earthly home so cozy. She concluded:

> Then straight I 'gin my heart to chide,
> And did thy wealth on earth abide?
> Didst fix thy hope on mold'ring dust?
> The arm of flesh didst make thy trust?
> Raise up thy thoughts above the sky
> That dunghill mists away may fly.
> Thou hast a house on high erect,
> Framed by that mighty Architect,
> With glory richly furnished,
> Stands permanent though this be fled.
> It's purchased and paid for too
> By Him who hath enough to do.
> A price so vast as is unknown
> Yet by His gift is made thine own;
> There's wealth enough, I need no more,

Farewell, my pelf, farewell my store.
The world no longer let me love,
My hope and treasure lies above.[18]

Like an earthly house, our heavenly home is a place of charm, rest, and fellowship; but it is beautiful beyond compare, paid off—so no one needs to work—and belongs to us because of the amazing fact that we have been welcomed into God's family. Thus, Bradstreet may have lost the lesser, but she didn't—never could—lose the greater, the real meaning and substance of "home." Her connection to her earthly house "transcends a simple attachment to things" because such "feelings about her home" are "intimately tied to" her faith—they are tied to her eternal home.[19] You see, the concept and reality of home was not invented by human beings; it was created by God.

Four Flowers and a Tree

Yet, this trial—and the resilience required to bounce back from it—would pale in comparison to the untimely deaths of Bradstreet's grandchildren and daughter-in-law. These were severe tragedies. Though the rates of women and children dying in childbirth and the early death of children in general were much higher than they are now and death was a constant reality before the faces of the New England immigrants, neither of these truths made an early death any less distressing. In fact, despite death rates, children were still "considered . . . to be the means of providing long-lasting and perpetual legacy."[20] Thus, though the danger of death during birth was real (so that not only infants died but mothers also prepared to die), it was still a shocking event that resonated deep within the soul of each parent, each sibling, each grandparent.[21] More than this, it was the women—the "childbearers and childrearers"—who were "particularly vulnerable to the psychological stress of high mortality."[22] Such expectations and anxieties are seen clearly in Bradstreet's grief poems, as the sense of frustration, exhaustion, and dejection grows heavier with each death. Yet, as her despondency grew so did her faith rise to the challenge of affirming God's good character and plans, not in spite of her love for her family but because of it.

The first death came with eighteen-month-old Elizabeth. As Bradstreet said goodbye to Elizabeth, she mourned but did not despair. It seemed relatively easy (at least compared to the later deaths) to believe that they did not own Elizabeth, God did, and he was now taking her to her eternal home, which meant there could be an end to their tears. Bradstreet wrote:

Farewell fair flower that for a space was lent,
Then ta'en away unto eternity.
Blest babe, why should I once bewail thy fate,
Or sigh thy days so soon were terminate,
Since thou art settled in an everlasting state.[23]

Here, Bradstreet brings to bear her theological beliefs about children and heaven on this horrible event. First, she recognizes that kids are a gift from God and ultimately belong to him, though parents have the privilege of being stewards of this gift during their time on earth. In another poem she wrote when her son Samuel (Elizabeth's father) had travelled to England, we see this theology in more detail. Bradstreet prayed,

Thou mighty God of sea and land,
I here resign into Thy hand
The son of prayers, of vows, of tears,
The child I stayed for many years.
Thou heard'st me then and gav'st him me;
Hear me again, I give him Thee.
He's mine, but more, O Lord, Thine own,
For sure Thy grace on him is shown.[24]

In other words, Bradstreet affirms that God is the Creator and controller of the whole earth and all of life and that he gave her Samuel (her firstborn) in response to her prayers to become a mother, so that though there is a real sense in which she can say Samuel belongs to her, he belongs first and foremost to God. Samuel came from God and will go back to God at the end of his life.

Further, in her other poems, Bradstreet affirmed that heaven was a place where there is no darkness, sickness, emotional pain, or moral failing—not even a memory of these—but only beauty, joy, and holiness. Thus, though Elizabeth was gone, she was not only with God, the one who made her, but with him in a beautiful place, where she did not know any disappointments.

Bradstreet continues her poem for Elizabeth by likening her death to the unnatural uprooting of a new plant as compared to the natural death of an old plant, and believed that such an event was the direct intervention of God to change his typical ordering of things. She reasoned:

By nature trees do rot when they are grown,
And plums and apples thoroughly ripe do fall,

And corn and grass are in their season mown,
And time brings down what is both strong and tall.
But plants new set to be eradicate,
And buds new blown to have so short a date,
Is by His hand alone that guides nature and fate.[25]

In other words, though this unnatural occurrence is surely difficult to accept, it is made easier by knowing for certain that God did it, and he did it on purpose. Thus, by drawing on her theological beliefs about children, heaven, and, at the end of the poem, providence, Bradstreet finds a sense of peace for herself and her family.

Unfortunately, Elizabeth was simply the beginning, and a whirlwind of deaths would hit the family a few years later, one right after the other. It was summertime when Samuel's daughter Anne—no doubt named after her grandma—passed away at three and a half years old. This second loss shook Bradstreet out of whatever peace she had found regarding Elizabeth's fate. She said:

With troubled heart and trembling hand I write,
The heavens have changed to sorrow my delight.[26]

Then, Bradstreet scolds herself for not properly learning the lesson that Anne too was lent, not owned, crying,

How oft with disappointment have I met,
When I on fading things my hopes have set.
Experience might 'fore this have made me wise,
To value things according to their price.
Was ever stable joy yet found below?

Or perfect bliss without mixture of woe?
I knew she was but a withering flower,
That's here today, perhaps gone in an hour;
Like as a bubble, or the brittle glass,
Or like a shadow turning as it was.
More fool then I to look on that was lent
As if mine own, when thus impermanent.[27]

Yet, though this event—the death of a child lent from the Lord—was the same, this *child* was not the same. The grief had to be felt all over again for this special person. In fact, Bradstreet not only recognized the individuality of all her children and grandchildren by naming them and saying particular things about them throughout her family poems, but also wrote a meditation about children in general that recognized the uniqueness of a child's temperament—even different than his or her siblings—and the importance of matching parenting styles to that temperament, using "salt" for some and "sugar" for others.[28] Thus, though little Anne had a similar fate to her sister Elizabeth, she deserved to be remembered in her own poem, grieved as her own person.

In the end, Bradstreet found the strength to bring together all her beliefs again and thus came to the same conclusion that she did about Elizabeth—that this child is now happy and with God. However, Bradstreet also adds another piece of the puzzle. Not only is little Anne with God, but Bradstreet herself will soon be with them. And, since this was a poem for her family, each member could then place themselves in the position of the narrator—including poor Samuel—which meant that all of them would reunite in heaven one day. Bradstreet writes,

Farewell dear child, thou ne'er shall come to me,
But yet a while, and I shall go to thee;
Mean time my throbbing heart's cheered up with this:
Thou with my Savior art in endless bliss.[29]

Sadly, this was still not the end of the Bradstreet family's trials. In the autumn of the same year, Samuel's son Simon, who was probably named after his grandfather and expected to carry on the family's heritage, died "but a month and one day old."[30] Bradstreet explains that though they were not together for long, this did nothing to lessen the blow. She opens her poem,

No sooner came, but gone, and fall'n asleep,
Acquaintance short, yet parting caused us weep.[31]

She continues on, portraying this third flower—merely an unopened bud—with the two other flowers, which had partly blossomed, writing,

Three flowers, two scarcely blown, the last i' th' bud,
Cropt by th' Almighty's hand; yet is He good.[32]

But by now, it was getting hard to affirm God's goodness. So Bradstreet confronts her doubts head on by speaking openly about them and attempting to convince her family to join her in falling prostrate before God, thrusting such faithless thoughts into the ground. She proclaims,

With dreadful awe before Him let's be mute,
Such was His will, but why, let's not dispute,
With humble hearts and mouths put in the dust,
Let's say He's merciful as well as just.[33]

Yet, they must not only silence their doubts about God's goodness by burying them, declaring they are dead, but also by remembering that part of his good gift is everlasting life. Thus, Bradstreet's faith both showed grave respect to God *and* recognized that it is right to soothe our pain by thinking of the promises he makes to give us good things that will bring us joy. She consoles,

He will return and make up all our losses,
And smile again after our bitter crosses.
Go pretty babe, go rest with sisters twain;
Among the blest in endless joys remain.[34]

The loss of a child or grandchild seems almost unreal, and it's hard to think of something that could be worse. But another death of an older, key family member would hit the Bradstreet family the next fall, as Samuel's wife, Mercy, passed away at twenty-eight years old. Now, Bradstreet protests: Why is she still alive when Elizabeth, Anne, Simon, and Mercy are all dead? Has she only survived so that there would be someone to sing at their funerals? She gives voice to her bitterness and confusion when she begins her poem:

And live I still to see relations gone,
And yet survive to sound this wailing tone;

Ah, woe is me, to write thy funeral song,
Who might in reason yet have lived long.[35]

This is not how it was supposed to be. Years earlier, Bradstreet had written a tribute to her own mother saying she had "lived to see" all her grandchildren and left a "blessed memory" with them when she passed.[36] Bradstreet would later expand this idea and apply it to her own life in the poem she wrote about raising her eight children, expressing her hope that not only them but also their children would hear stories of their old grandma after she passed away. She daydreamed:

Meanwhile my days in tunes I'll spend,
Till my weak lays with me shall end.
In shady woods I'll sit and sing,
And things that past to mind I'll bring.
Once young and pleasant, as are you,
But former toys (no joys) adieu.
My age I will not once lament,
But sing, my time so near is spent,
And from the top bough take my flight
Into a country beyond sight,
Where old ones instantly grow young,
And there with seraphims set song;
No seasons cold, nor storms they see;
But spring lasts to eternity.
When each of you shall in your nest
Among your young ones take your rest,
In chirping languages oft them tell,

You had a dame that loved you well,
That did what could be done for young,
And nursed you up till you were strong,
And 'fore she once would let you fly,
She showed you joy and misery;
Taught what was good, and what was ill,
What would save life, and what would kill.
Thus gone, amongst you I may live,
And dead, yet speak, and counsel give:
Farewell, my birds, farewell adieu,
I happy am, if well with you.[37]

But this was not to be, at least for Samuel's immediate family. It seems *she* would be the one left to tell the stories about *them*, so many taken while they were too young.

Yet, the loss of this dream for Samuel's future spouse and children is nowhere near as bad as the real thing, for in losing Mercy, Bradstreet not only lost the idea of her eldest's happy family but also a specific, real human being she was close to. So Bradstreet mourns both the loss of her friend as well as the wife of her son Samuel and mother of his children, and thus has a double portion of grief. She cries,

I saw the branches lopped the tree now fall,
I stood so nigh, it crushed me down withal.
My bruised heart lies sobbing at the root,
That thou, dear son, hath lost both tree and fruit.
Thou, then on seas sailing to foreign coast,
Was ignorant what riches thou hadst lost.

But ah too soon those heavy tidings fly,
To strike thee with amazing misery;
Oh how I sympathize with thy sad heart,
And in thy griefs still bear a second part.[38]

Bradstreet then gives voice to her son's greater grief by expressing the intimate connection between him and Mercy, saying that when Mercy's body died she had actually already gone because she was with Samuel in spirit, who was away in Jamaica at the time. Bradstreet explains to her son,

I lost a daughter dear, but thou a wife,
Who loved thee more (it seemed) than her own life.
Thou being gone, she longer could not be,
Because her soul she'd sent along with thee.
One week she only passed in pain and woe,
And then her sorrows all at once did go.[39]

But, there's more. We then discover the gut-wrenching fact that Mercy had just given birth, and that her child also died. Bradstreet continued:

A babe she left before she soared above,
The fifth and last pledge of her dying love,
Ere nature would, it hither did arrive,
No wonder it no longer did survive.[40]

This is a bleak picture. But Bradstreet finds one small light to end her poem on Mercy—that at least she is in her eternal home with her children who had died young, and that she left one behind, a little Mercy, to be with the rest of the family:

> So with her children four, she's now at rest,
> All freed from grief (I trust) among the blest;
> She one hath left, a joy to thee and me,
> The heavens vouchsafe she may so ever be.[41]

Then, Bradstreet turns to Samuel one final time—the child she had asked for and received, prayed for God to protect and he did—to reaffirm that this fate is from God, who has their best interest in mind. She reassured,

> Cheer up, dear son, thy fainting bleeding heart,
> In Him alone that caused all this smart;
> What though thy strokes full sad and grievous be,
> He knows it is the best for thee and me.[42]

Thus, without ignoring the extreme sadness that Samuel would have felt, Bradstreet reminds him that not only does God reign over all the occurrences in their lives, but that he is also working everything to their good.

Since Bradstreet was with her daughter-in-law when she died and had emotionally guided the family through the deaths of Mercy and Samuel's children, it seems natural that Bradstreet and her husband became little Mercy's permanent guardians, educating and raising her while Samuel was in Jamaica.[43] And for all of the family, Bradstreet formalized the precious memories of their loved ones in her prayer-poems that they could read whenever they felt the need to remember them and what had passed and to anticipate their future together.

The Work of My Family

In a journal entry written toward the end of her life, Bradstreet recalled how God helped her recover from a recent illness, saying he had "given me many a respite and some ability to perform the duties I owe to Him and the work of my family."[44] This reference to her labor in the home may not strike us today, but in Bradstreet's time, "women's traditional household routine was taken for granted by the larger society, not usually distinguished with the term 'work.' Childbearing, childrearing, and house-wifery were not considered real occupations, but were merely the things that women did."[45]

Yet, Bradstreet knew better than this. Her poems put on display her work of teaching, supporting, and caring for her children and grandchildren and their home. Though such gifts of life and love are created by God and belong to him (only being lent to us for a time) and though they all eventually turn to dust—sometimes much sooner than we expect—they are also imbued with spiritual, everlasting value and are thus worth working for because they are directly connected to the eternal life we will have together and with God. In fact, the very act of working in the family is godlike. In her letter to her children, Bradstreet said that one of the realities that convinced her that God was real when she had doubts of his existence was his "daily providing for this great household upon the earth."[46]

Such family work can be difficult, and when we invest in it we will surely experience many emotional ups and downs, like

Bradstreet did, feeling wholehearted joy when welcoming a new family member and a fainting, bleeding, or throbbing in our bruised heart when tragedy strikes. But we should not ignore these feelings or treat them as irrational or faithless. Rather, we should follow them—with all their unresolved tensions—into candid lament and praise to God, for when we do, he will show us the way to eternity, where all our emotions are sorted out and our family and home are waiting.

Lady Brilliana Harley

Matriarch as Physician,
Using Spiritual Conversation

OUT OF ALL OF THE SPECIAL pieces of literature in this book, it's the letters of this chapter that win the prize for most shocking. If you've ever read Jane Austen's novels, you'll know what I mean when I say that the stakes are high when a heroine receives a letter. Remember when Elizabeth spots Mr. Darcy in the park and he catches up to her to give her a note? Or when Marianne finally receives a response from Willoughby after waiting for what feels like forever? Or when Captain Wentworth slinks back into the drawing room to discreetly leave a folded paper for Anne? We instinctively hold our breath when a letter arrives.

Such is the case in the story of Lady Brilliana Harley (*bap.* 1598, *d.* 1643), a gentlewoman in Herefordshire who defended her household against a siege led by the king's royalists during the English Civil War, not by bedecking herself in armor and mounting a horse (though she did live in a castle), but through valiant letter-writing.[1] She not only refused to follow direct orders from the royalist commander but even responded to letters from the king himself, impressively mustering up the courage to claim the rights of citizenship and ownership in unconventional ways for a woman at this time even though her correspondents included the most powerful man in the country.[2] On top of this, she also "organized an efficient intelligence service" from the castle by sharing information in hopes it would "counter movements of the local royalists" and ordered what would be a successful attack on nearby royalists, thus acting as a "commander in every sense of the word."[3] If you thought Beaumont, Hutchinson, Rich, or Bradstreet had the most guts, it's because you hadn't yet met Harley.

Harley the Protector

Yet, Harley's great legacy in letters is not only found in this political maneuvering but also in the care she extended to her eldest son Edward (affectionately called "Ned") up until her death. Though not as awe-inspiring as her siege letters, her day-to-day conversations with her son make up about half of a four-hundred-piece collection and give us the opportunity to take a peek into the mind of a woman who was known for her tenacious leadership during crisis and exceptional devotion to God.

Brilliana—unique in many ways—received her unique name from Brill, Netherlands (being born in the English garrison there) and was educated in Latin, French, history, and the Bible.[4] As she grew up, she took on the parliamentarian and Puritan values of her family and would later marry a man who saw the world in the same way, Sir Robert Harley, joining him at Brampton

Bryan Castle in Herefordshire. In a neighborhood largely made up of royalists, this couple was known throughout town for their strong convictions, and together they raised seven children— Edward (Ned), Robert, Thomas, Brilliana, Dorothy, Margaret, and Elizabeth (who died young).

Thus, when it was time for Ned to go to college, they sent him to study at Magdalen Hall in Oxford because it employed Puritan tutors. While he was away, Harley wrote to him "at least once a week . . . for five years," dispensing spiritual advice about staying close to God, emotional support regarding his worldly endeavors, and even material goods like food and medicine in order to continue caring for him and remind him of home.[5] Such letter writing was not uncommon among mothers of this era, but Harley was unique for her intellectual interests, as seen in the fact that she usually exchanged views with Ned and others about politics and religion instead of "cheese," as one correspondent put it.[6] Though life was not without its trials, as Harley suffered from bouts of illness and missed having Ned at home, this seemed to be a sweet season for both of them. He was happy at school, and because of this, she was happy.

Sadly, this peaceful time would come to a grinding halt as the country approached the verge of civil war. At this point, everything changed for Harley's family as they were scattered and faced many dangers. Her husband went to London to attend Parliament, Ned was placed "in charge of a troop of horse," and Robert joined him so that both brothers were "frequently in active combat."[7] Meanwhile, young Brilliana "was stranded in London where she had been visiting relatives," and "Harley and the younger children were at Brampton Bryan with other members of a local godly community in an area largely controlled by royalists."[8] Unfortunately, Harley and her three youngest could not travel to reunite with the others in London—they were stuck.[9] Thus, to protect her household and the Puritans who sought refuge in her castle, Harley "defensively . . . filled the moat, stockpiled weapons and took in an armed band," which effectively transformed the castle into a kind of garrison.[10]

Soon after, Harley received a "formal demand to surrender Brampton . . . to the royalists" and boldly "refused."[11] Despite such imminent danger, Harley dug her heels in and responded with savvy—even fierceness!—to letters from the royalist commander and the king of England. However, her situation continued to worsen as "cannonballs battered the walls and supplies ran dangerously short"—the royalists were trying to starve them out.[12] Jacqueline Eales explains that at this point, the fifty musketeers and fifty civilians, as well as Harley's children and her friends, were all suffering inside Brampton: "Conditions were extremely uncomfortable and dangerous . . . the cattle, sheep, and horses were plundered; the mills, town houses, and barns were all burnt to the ground and the castle was extensively damaged by continual bombardment with cannon and small shot."[13] One person had died, and others had been wounded. However, against all odds, Harley exhibited great physical courage, which rubbed off on the others, and successfully thwarted the siege.[14]

Spend Your Health to the Glory of God

Such victory must have felt good; Harley accomplished what she had set out to do. Yet her successful defense was most valuable not because it was a protection of Brampton Bryan Castle itself but because it was a protection of the precious life she had created with her family and community within its walls. As we'll see in her letters to Ned, these connections were more ordinary than her extraordinary defense of the castle, but their relational riches ran deep and far and wide. When we come to these letters, we are observing the fruit of over a decade of togetherness.

As one might expect with any close relationship, Harley recorded whatever came to mind when writing to Ned—from local and national news to family updates to items she was hoping to order from Oxford. But, most often, her mind was on spiritual things, including the spiritual well-being of her son. Thus, Harley had intentional discussions about religion with him (what the Puritans called "conferencing"), encouraging him to live for God, sharing her own religious experiences, and connecting him to the community of faith.

Perhaps more than anything else, Harley's most constant refrain to Ned was "devote yourself to God." Harley was an expert in devotion. She had studied the Bible, served God, suffered through trials, and come out the other side a blessed woman. Thus, she continually prompted Ned to keep the Sabbath, read God's word, and spend time in prayer, all out of a sincere love for God himself. Not long after Ned left for Oxford, she reminded him, "We must feed upon the word of God, which, when we have done, we must not let it lie idle, but we must be diligent in exercising of what we know, and the more we practice the more we shall know. Dear Ned, let nothing hinder you from performing constant, private duties of praying and reading."[15]

For Harley, fulfilling one's duties to God took commitment and work; it was not something that one could simply think good thoughts about and hope it happened. She prayed that Ned would have a "strong and lively soul, always active in the ways of grace" and told him to "grow not slack," "stir up yourself to exercise yourself," and "spend all your strength and health to the glory of your God."[16]

Yet, as important as these behaviors were, the state of one's heart was just as vital to true religion. Thus, Harley also prompted Ned to draw near to God and sincerely love him, saying things like, "Keep a fresh desire after the sincere milk of the word," and "Keep [your] heart close with God . . . that you may remember your Creator now, in the days of your youth, that in . . . old age you . . . may say, Lord, remember your servant who has always desired to serve you."[17]

But, what makes the love of God really beautiful is that it is not a feigned, forced kind of love, solely based on duty and propped up by one's own feelings and actions. Rather, it is genuine and reciprocal, in that because God loves us first and his love is so entrancing, it draws us to him and fills us up, making us instinctively yet willingly love him in return. Thus, Harley instructed, "Since he has loved you, show your love to him," and prayed, "The Lord bless you and make you grow in the love of Jesus Christ, that that love may be all in all in you."[18] And in the middle of her letters, she would spontaneously exclaim, "O that we could but see the depth of that love of God in Christ to us: then surely love would constrain us to serve the Lord with all our hearts most willingly," and "O it is a sweet thing to open our hearts to our God as to a friend."[19] Upon sending Ned to Magdalen Hall, Harley could have simply assumed he would follow suit in the example of devotion being laid out for him.

But she didn't—she made sure to check in and remind him that devotion required an intimate, personal interaction that could not be replaced with a dupe, no matter which family you came from or which school you went to.

Knowing he would need more than these nudges to stay on the right path, Harley also taught Ned about what hinders devotion to God, such as worldly distractions, seeing other people sin, and giving into temptation ourselves. In her very first letter she counseled, "You are now in a place of more varieties then when you were at home; therefore take heed it take not up your thoughts as much as to neglect that constant service you owe to your God."[20] As time went on, she again reminded Ned, "Be still watchful over yourself, so that custom in seeing and hearing of vice does not abate your distaste of it."[21] Yet, Harley claimed that the most dangerous hindrance to devotion is our own sin. She simultaneously warned, "Rather die than sin against your gracious and holy God," and comforted, "We have so gracious a God that nothing can put a distance between him and our souls but sin."[22]

But how does a believer do all of this in real life? Harley did not leave Ned to figure out the practicalities of devotion on his own but, like other physicians of the soul (as the Puritans were sometimes called), she also shared remedies for these spiritual ailments. Above all, she encouraged Ned to take a good look at his heart on a "daily" basis, saying things like put your "eye" on your "soul" and "be watchful over your heart, that nothing steal away your affections from your God."[23] In one letter, she gave him specific instructions for how to engage in such self-examination, a common practice among the Puritans but one that we are often unfamiliar with today. She explained:

1. Think over the company you have been in, and what your discourse was, and how you found yourself affected, including in the discourses of religion;
2. Observe what knowledge you were able to express and with what affection to it, and where you find yourself to come short, labor to repair that want;
   (a) if it be in knowledge of any point, read something that may inform you in what you find you know not;
   (b) if the fault be in affections, that you find a weariness in that discourse of religion, go to God and beg of him new affections to love those things which by nature we cannot love.
3. After discourse, call to mind whether you have been too apt to take exceptions, or whether any have provoked you, and examine yourself, how you took it.[24]

Then, she continued on to show why such self-examination is necessary, reasoning,

I think it is the best way to be acquainted with our own hearts, for we know not what is in us until occasion and temptation draws out that matter which lays quiet; and in a due observation, we shall find at last, in what we are proud, in what fearful, and what will vex and eat our hearts with care and grief.[25]

Finally, to drive home her point and convince Ned that devoting his life to God was the most worthwhile thing he could do with it, Harley opened her life to him by recalling her personal experience. She shared:

> And my dearest, believe this from me, that there is no sweetness in anything in this life that can be compared to the sweetness in the service of our God, and this I thank God, I can say experimentally; I have had health and friends and company in variety, and there was a time that what could I have said I wanted? Yet in all that there was a trouble, and that which gave me peace was serving of my God . . . I have had a time of sickness, and weakness, and the loss of friends, and as I may say, the gliding away of all those things I took most comfort in, in this life.[26]

She continued on, saying that if she placed these two conditions side by side—when she had worldly comforts and when she did not—she would prefer not having them because they were inadequate and fleeting, but the comfort she received from God during a trial was satisfying and long-lasting.

More than this personal connection and satisfaction, Harley believed that such outward—and even inward—devotion should not only be enjoyed on an individual basis but also with the church and the family. This is seen when she advised, "Be constant in holy duties" and immediately added, "Let public and private go together."[27] She also mentioned what she, her husband, and the other children were doing in Ned's absence, and invited him to join with them in the same practices at the same time so that though they were physically apart, they may be spiritually together in the Lord. For example, she once said:

I hope in a special manner, we shall remember you at the fast; and, dear Ned, think upon that day, how your father is used to spend it, that so you may have like affections to join with us. Let your desire be often presented before your God that day; and the Lord, who only hears prayers, hear us all.[28]

Because of this, Harley saw her prayers and the prayers of her son meeting in heaven before the throne of God and told Ned that praying "is the best thing that we can do, one for another."[29] No wonder she and Ned were so close!

If You Be Well, I Count It upon My Own Score

Harley considered this kind of active, sincere, watchful, and communal devotion to God to be the center of Christian living. Yet, such devotion also affected other parts of life on earth. Thus, Harley not only offered guidance concerning spiritual things but also intellectual and emotional support as Ned navigated the world on his own. In addition to encouraging him to study Scripture—as she had done since he was old enough to read, ensuring he received his first Bible at the age of five—she also sent him books so they could discuss their contents together, analyzed current events with him, and professed, "I desire you may have that true health in your soul of a sound mind, that so in these days of wavering and doubting you may hold the truth."[30]

Further, knowing Ned was a normal human being who experienced many feelings and needed a listening ear, she also let him vent his worries, gave practical advice, and prompted him to trust God. On one occasion, she told him that if he ever had any important visitors that he should respect them but also to not feel inferior, be "put out of" himself, or "lose" himself because he was also part of a respectable family; according to Harley, this wasn't the vice of sinful pride but the wisdom of simply knowing yourself and knowing others.[31] Similarly, she told him to not look down on others if he was wearing expensive clothes but they weren't and to not be embarrassed if he was underdressed.

As Ned first experienced the stresses of school, Harley also became his greatest cheerleader. Once, when he feared that his beloved tutor might be leaving Oxford to teach elsewhere, Harley empathized with and comforted him. She affirmed how valuable his tutor was by saying that Ned had not simply found a good instructor but one who was suitable to his heart, and she validated his anxiety by saying, "I cannot blame you to fear the losing of him" since finding a mentor with a similar view of life is rare and should be cherished.[32] Yet, she also reminded Ned of God's providence and how, through all of the ups and downs in life, she wrote, "God still provided for you; and so I trust he will do still."[33] Similarly, Harley sent good wishes after Ned's exams, saying, "I hope your mind and tongue were in good tune," and then assured him, "If you should not do as well as you desire, yet let it not discourage you."[34]

Perhaps most importantly, as political tensions rose, Harley instructed Ned to think about spiritual warfare, remember that God kept him safe, and continue to act in an honorable way, writing, "When it is in your power show kindness to [those who threaten us], for they must be overcome so. . . . You and I must forgive them."[35] Johanna Harris insightfully explains that, in the seventeenth century, letters had the power to "make the recipient feel a part of something bigger," provide connection "to the anchor of home," and bestow "dignity" by enacting a shared "moral code," all of which had "therapeutic" effects.[36] In other words, by connecting Ned not only to herself but also his biological and spiritual heritage, Harley was grounding him in his own identity and thus promoting his mental and emotional well-being.

Yet, I would be remiss if this chapter painted the picture of an exacting, perfectionist, or distant Harley in your mind. If you read these hundreds of letters for yourself, you would see that the general spirit of her entire collection of letters is that of free-flowing love, not detailed instruction. Though Harley's counsel to live before the face of God permeates her letters, it was always shaped and softened by her continually telling Ned how much she loved him and how much she appreciated his love.

For example, she often expressed how much she missed him, nudged him to write to her more often "though it be 2 or 3 words," received so much joy from his letters that it improved her health, and wrote back as much as humanly possible, sometimes scribbling and running out of paper.[37] If mail was being sent, she would write a letter at the last minute even though she had not planned to, simply in order to tell him for the millionth time that she loved him. In fact, she told Ned, "Could I hear from you and send to you every day, I should be glad."[38] It was easy for her to send so many letters because he was always on her mind—writing was simply putting her thoughts to paper. And when she hadn't heard from him in a while, she hoped he was well and justified her desire to hear from him by saying, "Love is watchful."[39]

Harley also appreciated how Ned showed "childlike expressions of love" in writing to her, caring about her health, desiring to know her thoughts, supporting her and his father, remembering her birthday, shopping for her in Oxford, and diligently updating her on news (which was especially important when political rumors were being spread).[40] It was precisely because she knew that Ned loved her letters that she wrote so often. Though Ned was her dependent who she gave advice and nurture to, he was also becoming an adult who was able to show similar care in return. Echoing the voices of all moms everywhere, Harley once told Ned that her doctor "observed I neglected myself," but Ned's continual inquiries about her health and reminders about remedies gave her the space to remember, speak freely about, and take care of her own body.[41] In fact, it seems that the chronic illness Harley was suffering was related to menstruation, which shows she was not embarrassed to talk openly about specific bodily ailments with Ned, even when such ailments were private.[42]

Surely, the best parts of her letters are the ones that reveal their shared life force. On the one hand, Brilliana often testified to her closeness with Ned by saying things like, "If you be well, I count it upon my own score, and think myself so."[43] She valued his life as her own, and prayed for the same blessings for him that she did for herself. On the other hand, she lamented the limits of letters, wishing that she was with him so that she could speak more freely than she could in writing and even that she was the letter carrier herself or could be as easily sent as a letter so that she could see her son in person. Perhaps most poignantly, she wrote in what would be her final correspondence with Ned of her deep longing to be with him and signed off in her usual manner:

How much I long to see you I cannot express, and if it be possible, in part meet my desires in desiring, in some measure

as I do, to see me . . . I pray God bless you and give me the
comfort of seeing you, for you are the comfort of

Your most affectionate mother, Brilliana Harley.[44]

Thus, Brilliana's and Ned's letters were so much more than just
pen on paper—they were pieces of themselves given to each other,
physical representations of their shared love that they could cher-
ish when they were apart.

When You Are Ill, My Prayers Are More for You

Maybe this spiritual and emotional care seems enough to support
dear Ned. But Harley did not stop there. You see, her letters were
not only vehicles for words expressing her own heart and written
in her own hand, but also a means of sending food, medicine,
clothing, and other items on a regular basis. And, just as her advice
for godly living was made holistic with an application to Ned's
whole person and affirmations of love, so were her gifts given not
just for his body but also his spirit.

For example, Harley's care packages often acted as reminders of
home. In one of her first letters to Ned she wrote in a post note,
"I have sent you a cake, which I hope you will eat in memory of
Brampton."[45] She also ate in memory of him, writing on one occasion that since Ned left home, his father had wanted strawberry
butter, so "in memory of [Ned that] day" she had her servant
make it and then sent some to Ned with her latest letter update.[46]

Harley put this same thought and intention into sending Ned
medicine, oftentimes not even waiting for him to get sick. She
once sent him "juice of licorice" to keep handy for when he had
a cold and, after he was treated by a doctor for eye problems, sent

him eye water to prevent any negative long-term effects and to help him preserve his eyesight.[47] Such close attention was nothing new for Harley; she had been taking care of Ned since he was born, as seen in her earlier letters to her husband, Robert, wherein she recorded the times that Ned was teething, had a cold, and took his first steps—the licorice and eye water were simply a continued outworking of her undying motherly love.[48]

We may think she had done everything she possibly could, but Harley continued on, using this opportunity to help Ned stay positive, tell him about the time she had eye problems, and remind him of spiritual truths. She affirmed:

> Though I am not afraid of your eyes, yet I cannot but pity them . . . I know it to be a great pain; for once I had sore eyes, and when by experience we feel how tender the eye is, we may call to mind how sensible God is of all the wrongs which are done his children, when he is pleased to say that they who touch his children touch the apple of his eye: therefore woe be to those that are so bold; and happy are those that are in that account with the Lord.[49]

Not surprisingly, when Ned neglected to tell her about a particular illness, Harley scolded him, like most moms would. On one occasion she asked,

> But, my dear Ned, are you willing to hide your being ill from me, who only desires to partake with you in all that befalls you? My dear Ned, when you are ill, my prayers are more for you, and the Lord, I hope, will hear me in his Son. . . . Dear Ned,

be never unwilling that I should know how it is with you; for none has a more tender apprehension of it then myself.[50]

With this letter she sent some more remedies, and three days later she sent another letter, empathizing with his pain. She wrote, "My dear Ned, nothing can more please me then to have a sympathy with you, therefore not to know how it is with you would be a torture to me; and when you are not well, sorrow is a thousand times more pleasing to me then to be merry."[51] And, like she did when he had eye problems, Harley continued on to turn his thoughts to spiritual truths, telling him to make the most of this trial for the good of his soul.

Just like her letters, Harley's gifts connected Ned to his family and community. On one occasion, she sent Ned a purse full of money in order to spur on thoughts of her because she always thought of him. She explained, "I have sent you a little purse with some small money in it, all the pence I had, that you may have a penny to give a poor person and a pair of gloves; not that I think you have not better in Oxford, but that you may sometimes remember her, that seldom has you out of my thoughts."[52] She also sent him her own watch, which previously belonged to her father—who was known for his religious devotion—and instructed Ned to wear it until he could get his own, advising, "Love it better than you would another watch" because of its sentimental value.[53] Even his sisters sent him small tokens through their mother's letters, and his brother Thomas once acted as Harley's amanuensis. All in all, Harley was truly willing to go to any length to provide for Ned, even during the siege when she could hardly provide for herself, writing, "My dear Ned, if you want anything that I can help you to, I pray you send to me; and be sure I will want myself, before you shall."[54]

Yet, lest I make it seem like Ned was spoiled rotten, it is important to tell you that Harley also asked for items in return, as well as for Ned's help in dispersing gifts to others. For example, she often asked Ned to look for specific items in Oxford that would be less expensive there than in Herefordshire. She once asked him, "If there be any good-looking glasses in Oxford, choose me one about the bigness of that I use to dress me in, if you remember it. I put it to your choice."[55] And a few months later, he sent some glasses. Though these transactions may seem insignificant, they further testify to the closeness of their relationship, as Harley asked for Ned's help not only to save money but also because he knew her preferences and she trusted his judgment. Thus, when he sent her a fabric pattern and she liked it, she recovered chairs in it and hoped he would enjoy seeing them the next time he came home.

More than this, Harley frequently asked Ned to pass on letters, food, and other items to extended family members (like cousins and uncles) as well as friends, which required him to correspond or even have face-to-face contact with them. Perhaps this personal connection is really what Harley was hoping to nurture. For example, she expressed her satisfaction that Ned spent time with her brother, who was far from God. And after she caught Ned's little brother Thomas weeping "in private" because he thought he had angered Ned, she coaxed Ned to write to him and attempted to stir his affections by reminding him that Tom "is the most like you, and loves you dearly."[56] Thus, by inspiring Ned to imitate her care, Harley effectively started a chain reaction of gift-giving and life-sharing throughout the family and their surrounding communities.

General Practitioners

Sadly, despite living such an influential life, Harley's time was cut short by the siege as she contracted a cold and died suddenly and unexpectedly before her home was surrendered during a second attack.[57] Yet, this wasn't really the end. All of the love that she had poured into Ned would culminate in his continuing her legacy of spiritual, emotional, and physical caretaking into his later years.

For the rest of his adult life, Ned continued to live out the heart religion taught him by his mother, energetically and sincerely devoting himself to God, just as she hoped he would. In fact, Richard Baxter described Ned as a "sober and truly religious man."[58] Even more tellingly, Ned's own son Edward "referred to [Ned's] habit throughout his life of constant reading of the scriptures," so that we may now say, "Brampton Bryan in [Ned's] time perhaps epitomized the ideal of the spiritual puritan household."[59] Ned also wrote to his wife's family members on her behalf and continued to write to his brother Thomas, advocated for nonconformists, and even repaired the chapel and park at Brampton Bryan Castle, where he lived out the rest of his days. Yet, perhaps most significantly, Ned himself expressed in a retrospect of his own life upon turning fifty years old, "Blessed be God! who has granted me favor in the affection of my father and my mother, who tenderly loved me, and wisely and carefully instructed and corrected me."[60] Why do you think we have Harley's hundreds of letters today? Because Ned, the recipient, kept them—each and every one.

Though we don't know exactly how Ned responded since his letters have been lost in time (perhaps being destroyed in Brampton Bryan Castle during the siege), it seems that, had he ever found himself wanting to get his mother's advice or be near to her, he would have had no hesitation or difficulty in doing so because she was so present in his life, always seeking to learn about what was going on with him and his evolving interests, feel with him as he experienced stress, worry, excitement, and pain, pay attention to him as a whole person, and teach him how to use theology to inform all of life. Further, by fashioning opportunities for Ned to do the same for others, she gave him the opportunity to fulfill his part in the Harleys' "natural role as leaders of county society."[61] Thus, her letters were not just the daily musings of one mother who lived four hundred years ago, but the record of an entire extended family and community, caring for each other spiritually, intellectually, emotionally, and physically, all spurred on by this one matriarch. So while we might feel tempted to devalue the thousands of acts of care we do for our many loved ones because, in and of themselves, they seem small, we must remember that the love that is given through them will live on in the ones who receive it. In some cases, even the tiny tokens we give may last many lifetimes, continuing not just a legacy of our own name but also of God's.

Conclusion

Spiritual Loving Care

One House

Surely, the five women we've listened to on our trip to the seventeenth century left a legacy that is worth remembering today. Though we're not sure if they ever met, we may now—with hindsight into their lives that even they didn't have and their captivating stories at the forefront of our minds—invite them over to have a conversation with us and each other about what it means to minister to our families using spiritual practices.

One God

Where does such ministry begin? I think all of these women would say that in order to bring your family, church, or community close to God, you first have to be close to God yourself. Indeed, these women's schedules were filled to the brim with, even dictated by, their use of spiritual practices that enabled them to be alone with God in order to pour out their hearts to him and listen to his response through Scripture and the Spirit. As I hope you've seen, they used lots of methods. There really wasn't one formula or one way of bringing them all together; they just lived their lives with God in a way that organically took a shape that was unique to them as individuals. They loved him, so they spent time with him—and that's really all there was to it! Thus, though they were zealous, they were neither extreme nor legalistic. Such practices were motivated by love and required a level of fun and creativity that is involved in any kind of close relationship.

Naturally, many of these disciplines were often used in solitude, so these women had to seek time alone. As Mary Rich and Brilliana Harley showed us, some aspects of devotion to God required getting away from the hustle and bustle of life—the busyness of dealing with family, work, and social events, including the sinful distractions that were sometimes wrapped up in them. Even in the midst of massive trials and tragedies, such as when Agnes Beaumont was preparing to speak to the jury or when Lucy Hutchinson was scrambling to provide for her children, these women generally found time to be quiet before God. Of course, sometimes such circumstances changed their habits for a time, like when Rich stopped meditating during the final months of her husband's life and right after his death. Like her diary shows us, sometimes they were just not physically able to have the kind of quality time with God that they wanted to. Yet, in general, these women prioritized being alone with him, in the sense that it was an essential part of their typical lifestyles. They knew this space was where God would meet them and they were committed to having a relationship with him, so they went there, day after day, simply to be together.

Overall, such devotional time was mentally, emotionally, and behaviorally constructive for them in that it influenced their perspectives on, and thus feelings about, the things they were going through at the time as well as the decisions they needed to make. By sitting down and taking a good, long, inquisitive look at their souls, the Bible, and the world around them, they were inspired to reaffirm their values—like charity, calmness, and community—and get to know themselves and what tempted them to accidentally fall into another path in life. Because they knew they were loved by God, they didn't lose their self-esteem when mistreated by others and even turned these trials into opportunities to show the reasonableness, virtues, and beauty of Christianity. And through sincerely expressing to God their true emotions—yes, all of them—when facing tragedy, they continued to stagger toward him in faith, knowing he could answer their deepest woes with his highest truths.

Most importantly, it was this quiet time alone that allowed them to simply be with God, which was the best place to be. Serving him was even sweeter than enjoying friendships and health; learning about him was the most worthwhile of all intellectual pursuits. And when friendships, health, and happiness were all but lost, God was the best company they could have asked for and always knew what was best for them, thus turning their times of sorrow into ones of well-being for their souls.

One Woman

"But where is the ministry part?" you ask. Well, right there. Don't you see it? The families and communities of these women were affected by their use of spiritual practices because it shaped these women to become who they were, including who they were to others. In other words, they developed a character that enabled them to nurture rich relationships with their families, churches, and communities because they had a rich relationship with God, the daily provider for this great household upon the earth.

In short, their prayers, meditations, and studies were applied to the lives of others—prayers for them, meditations about them, and studies concerning them. Yet, the effects of their spiritual maturity did not stop here—it also spilled over and into their worldly endeavors, helping them develop wisdom regarding the earthly aspects of child-rearing, homemaking, business management, community involvement, and healthy living. Those who cared for children and home applied their theology to everyday life in a way that enabled them to appreciate and listen to each unique child, respect their evolving relationship as these children grew up, comfort them later in life when facing change and loss, teach them how to care for their whole selves, and develop a divine appreciation for the earthly space and stuff they shared with them.

On a broader societal level, though they made sure to take care of themselves—their own health, finances, and personal relationships—and their families, they also holistically cared for their employees, the underprivileged and persecuted, and those in their communities who needed shelter during a crisis. And in addition to this personal and practical help—where the rubber really hits the road—they didn't skimp on preaching ideas that promoted the flourishing of all human beings, no matter who they are, by reminding those around them of God's infinite love and blessings, the dignity of those who may be despised by society, and the importance of forgiving enemies even in the heat of battle.

More than this, their devotion to God inspired the same kind of devotion in those around them—individuals in their families and communities took on the spiritual regimes of these women as their own, and they imitated the same heart-attitudes they saw in those daughters, mothers, wives, and grandmothers. Thus, their use of spiritual practices not only increased their oneness with God, but also each other. Each family—biological or spiritual—stayed together when they fasted, prayed, or served the poor.

Overall, though these women did not have the same credentials or draw the same crowd as the professional pastors they interacted with, we would be remiss to ignore the fact that their ministry was just as effective as their more famous counterparts: they were the female soul doctors of their time. In fact, their preaching was even more moving, their teaching more relevant, and their shepherding more empathetic when it came to their own family members, for it was all given in the context of their life together. They knew them as their loved ones and thus cared for them in ways that only they could know how.

Yet, despite all of the good this ministry brought, we have to say that this did not make their families, churches, or communities perfect. Like Hutchinson told us, the world is made up of sinners, the visible church has both hypocrites and true believers, and the converted—like these five women—still have weaknesses and indwelling sins. As Bradstreet discovered, you can't physically save your loved ones from death or emotionally save them from heartache because you don't control the universe or the human psyche. Rich and Beaumont would also tell us that you can't force religion or intimacy or even healthy ways of communication on others if they aren't personally willing to join you. Thus, while we have touching stories of uninterrupted affection like that of Brilliana and her dear Ned, we also have stories of heartbreaking estrangement that never seemed to reach a full resolution, like Mary and Charles. And even in the almost-too-good-to-be-true sagas of families like the Harleys, there are still tragedies. I'm not sure I'll ever get over the disappointment of knowing Brilliana died without getting to see Ned again. It's just not right!

One Story

There is something so deeply dissatisfying about not getting a proper conclusion, even if some parts of the story resolve. This is where the scope of happy endings in novels and movies stop short and the unique value of history can take us further in our attempt to use the stories of others to interpret our own. As much as I love a happily ever after, it can be a bit painful to see endings that are so happy they make you sad—sad that your family and friendships haven't turned out that way, sad to think of how great it would be if they did. But this is not a downside of true stories. Not only do they lack a perfect ending for their protagonists, but they really happened! They have a realness to them that not even the most real-feeling fantasy can imitate.

So now that we've reached the end of our experiment we can ask, what were the results? Overall, each woman had clogs and droopings that weighed them down, some of which could not be overcome. They loved but weren't loved in return. They wanted a happy family life but lost their family home and even family members. And at times, they were put on the outside of their entire community, made to feel truly alone.

Yet, what we can see now, with the privilege of history and looking back on the entire drama of each woman's life, is that their stories are ones of success! Sure, lots of bad things happened;

in fact, something in each of their stories—finances or relationships or health—was always going wrong. If it wasn't one thing, it was another thing, and sometimes many things at once. But through their devotion to God, they were able to impart to the people most important to them the greatest gift anyone could receive—spiritual loving care. And it is the same for us. In the midst of all the vanity, suffering, loose ends never tied up, and feelings of failure, the eternal love of God given to these women, returned to him, and distributed by them in their testimonies to Barbara, Samuel, Ned, and so many more, are sewn together into one big book of real-life love stories, ready for yours to be added.

Notes

Preface

1. Lucy Hutchinson, "My owne faith and attainment," in *The Works of Lucy Hutchinson*, vol. 2, *Theological Writings and Translations*, ed. Elizabeth Clarke, David Norbrook, Jane Stevenson (Oxford: Oxford University Press, 2018), 119.

Introduction

1. J. I. Packer, *A Quest for Godliness: The Puritan Vision of the Christian Life* (Wheaton, IL: Crossway, 1990), 29.

2. Packer explained, "Puritan thinkers generally agreed that divorce with right of remarriage was biblically permitted after adultery . . . [or] desertion, broadly interpreted to cover all behavior that nullified the matrimonial relationship in practice . . . with equal rights for men and women." Packer, *Quest for Godliness*, 269. In fact, the devout Calvinist mother of Lucy Hutchinson separated from and was later involved in a lawsuit with her second husband.

3. Lucy Hutchinson, "On the Principles of the Christian Religion," in *The Works of Lucy Hutchinson*, vol. 2, *Theological Writings and Translations*, ed. Elizabeth Clarke, David Norbrook, Jane Stevenson (Oxford: Oxford University Press, 2018), 193.

4. Packer, *Quest for Godliness*, 22.

5. Mary Rich and Raymond A. Anselment, *The Occasional Meditations of Mary Rich, Countess of Warwick* (Tempe, AZ: Arizona Center for Medieval and Renaissance Studies, 2009), 73. Used by permission.

6. For information about Lucy Hutchinson's, Anne Bradstreet's, and Brilliana Harley's engagement in the intellectual culture of their time,

see Johanna Harris and Elizabeth Scott-Baumann, eds., *The Intellectual Culture of Puritan Women, 1558–1680* (New York: Palgrave Macmillan, 2011). For examples of work that women did in the seventeenth century, see Sarah H. Mendelson, "Women and Work," in *A Companion to Early Modern Women's Writing*, ed. Anita Pacheco (Oxford: Blackwell, 2002).

7. Mendelson, "Women and Work," 70.

Chapter 1: Agnes Beaumont

1. *Oxford Dictionary of National Biography*, s.v. "Beaumont, Agnes (bap. 1652, d. 1720), religious autobiographer," by W. R. Owens, published in print and online Sept. 23, 2004, https://oxforddnb.com.

2. Vera J. Camden, introduction to *The Narrative of the Persecutions of Agnes Beaumont* (East Lansing, MI: Colleagues Press, 1992), 1.

3. Agnes Beaumont, *The Narrative and Persecutions of Agnes Beaumont*, ed. Vera J. Camden (East Lansing, MI: Colleagues Press, 1992), 43.

4. Beaumont, *Narrative*, 44.

5. Beaumont, *Narrative*, 44.

6. Anne Dunan-Page, *Grace Overwhelming: John Bunyan,* The Pilgrim's Progress, *and the Extremes of the Baptist Mind* (Oxford: Peter Lang, 2006), 79.

7. Rachel Adcock, *Baptist Women's Writings in Revolutionary Culture, 1640–1680* (Farnham: Ashgate, 2015), 33.

8. Beaumont, *Narrative*, 39; Adcock, *Baptist Women's Writings*, 41.

9. Though some modern readers may wonder if riding double on horseback was considered immodest, this does not seem to have been the interpretation of any main figures in this particular story. Beaumont's brother, who seems to be a mature Baptist believer and loving brother, was the first one to ask Bunyan to take her to church on horseback, and it is unlikely that Beaumont or Bunyan would have agreed to do something indecent (as they are both proved to be concerned with their godly reputations and proved to be innocent regarding several accusations in this text and others). Further, Beaumont's father had no problem with her riding behind another man, which was the original plan they had agreed to. Overall, the best interpretation of Beaumont's *Narrative* is one that accounts for all of the facts of the story as a whole and approaches Beaumont as an honest narrator who was in control of her own actions and admitted to her own failings. In this case, the most plausible reason that Beaumont's father and

the townspeople were taken aback by Beaumont's actions was that Bunyan, and Baptists in general, were social pariahs.

10. Beaumont, *Narrative*, 44.

11. Beaumont, *Narrative*, 45.

12. Beaumont, *Narrative*, 45.

13. Beaumont, *Narrative*, 46.

14. Beaumont, *Narrative*, 46.

15. Beaumont, *Narrative*, 47.

16. Beaumont, *Narrative*, 48.

17. Beaumont, *Narrative*, 49.

18. Beaumont, *Narrative*, 52.

19. Beaumont, *Narrative*, 56.

20. Beaumont, *Narrative*, 57.

21. Beaumont, *Narrative*, 58, 56.

22. Beaumont, *Narrative*, 61.

23. Beaumont, *Narrative*, 61.

24. Beaumont, *Narrative*, 61.

25. Beaumont, *Narrative*, 64.

26. Beaumont, *Narrative*, 65.

27. Beaumont, *Narrative*, 65.

28. Beaumont, *Narrative*, 65.

29. Beaumont, *Narrative*, 66.

30. Beaumont, *Narrative*, 69.

31. Patricia L. Bell, "Agnes Beaumont of Edworth," *Bunyan Studies* 10 (2001): 6.

32. Beaumont, *Narrative*, 74.

33. Beaumont, *Narrative*, 75–76.

34. Beaumont, *Narrative*, 80.

35. Beaumont, *Narrative*, 83.

36. Beaumont, *Narrative*, 83.

37. Beaumont, *Narrative*, 40, 47–48, 49, 60, 63, 64, 66, 68, 69, 73, 74, 83.

38. Adcock, *Baptist Women's Writings*, 33; Vera J. Camden, introduction to *The Narrative and Persecutions of Agnes Beaumont* (East Lansing, MI: Colleagues Press, 1992), 29.

39. Kathleen Lynch, "'Her Name Agnes': The Verifications of Agnes Beaumont's Narrative Ventures," *English Literary History* 67 (2000): 90.

40. *Oxford Dictionary of National Biography*, s.v. "Beaumont, Agnes," by Owens.

41. Beaumont, *Narrative*, 37–38.

Chapter 2: Lucy Hutchinson

1. Elizabeth Clarke, introduction to "On the Principles of the Christian Religion," in *The Works of Lucy Hutchinson*, vol. 2, *Theological Writings and Translations*, ed. Elizabeth Clarke, David Norbrook, Jane Stevenson (Oxford: Oxford University Press, 2018), 157. As the other chapters of this book illustrate, many writings from women in church history come in the form of letters, diary entries, and personal reflections. While still legitimate sources for exploring the theology (especially the spiritual theology) of lay people, Hutchinson's book—which is lengthier, more technical, and more systematic—stands out as the closest thing we have to a theological treatise written by a woman at this time.

2. Eales explains, "Although there were schools which admitted girls, they did not receive the intensely academic education reserved for their brothers, and, of course, they could not attend the universities or inns of court." Jacqueline Eales, *Puritans and Roundheads* (Glasgow: Harding Simpole Publishing, 2002), 25. Norbrook confirms that "as a woman [Hutchinson] had not been able to attend university or engage with many aspects of the masculine world of academic and clerical learning." David Norbrook, introduction to *Works of Lucy Hutchinson*, 2:xxxix.

3. Lucy Hutchinson, *Memoirs of the Life of Colonel Hutchinson* (Cambridge: Cambridge University Press, 2010), 17.

4. Susan Wiseman, *Conspiracy and Virtue: Women, Writing, and Politics in Seventeenth-Century England* (Oxford: Oxford University Press, 2007), 230.

5. Hutchinson, *Memoirs*, 43.

6. Hutchinson's historical record of events of the English Civil War, Interregnum, and Restoration is her most famous work, though she also wrote a lengthy poem on Genesis that is considered the first epic poem written by an Englishwoman. See Lucy Hutchinson, *Order and Disorder*, ed. David Norbrook (Oxford: Blackwell, 2001). This poem is sometimes referred to as Eve's version of Genesis. In addition to these original pieces (including her theological treatise), she translated into English a book by John Owen, a poem by Lucretius, and the Genevan chapter summaries of John Calvin's *Institutes of the Christian Religion*.

7. Though John Hutchinson had signed the warrant for the king's death, he was actually arrested for suspected involvement in a later plot against the monarchy and got sick while imprisoned.

8. *Oxford Dictionary of National Biography*, s.v. "Hutchinson [*née* Apsley], Lucy (1620–1681), poet and biographer," by David Norbrook,

published in print and online Sept. 23, 2004, https://www.oxford
dnb.com. David Norbrook, introduction to "Selections from the
Theological Notebook (DD/HU$_3$)," in *Works of Lucy Hutchinson*, 2:3.

9. Norbrook, introduction to "Selections from the Theological Notebook," 2:25.

10. The next three sections of this chapter have been adapted from Jenny-
Lyn de Klerk, "'Love toward all mankind in general we acknowledge
to be required of us': The Expanding and Elucidating of Loving One's
Neighbour in John Owen's and Lucy Hutchinson's Theology, Applied
to Their Involvement in Civil War" (PhD diss., Midwestern Baptist
Theological Seminary, 2020), 150–245.

11. See David Norbrook, introduction to *Works of Lucy Hutchinson*,
vol. 1: *The Translation of Lucretius*, part 1: *Introduction and Text*, ed.
Reid Barbour and David Norbrook (Oxford: Oxford University Press,
2012), xliii.

12. Gillian Wight, "The Material Muse: Anne Bradstreet in Manuscript
and Print," *Producing Women's Poetry* 57 (2013): 64–65.

13. Norbrook, introduction to *Works of Lucy Hutchinson*, 2:xv, xvii.

14. David Norbrook, "Lucy Hutchinson: Theology, Gender and Translation," *The Seventeenth Century* 30 (2015): 142.

15. Norbrook, introduction to *Works of Lucy Hutchinson*, 2:xix.

16. Lucy Hutchinson, "On the Principles of the Christian Religion," in
The Works of Lucy Hutchinson, 2:189, 193.

17. Hutchinson, "Principles of the Christian Religion," 2:189.

18. Hutchinson, "Principles of the Christian Religion," 2:189.

19. Hutchinson, "Principles of the Christian Religion," 2:191.

20. Hutchinson, "Principles of the Christian Religion," 2:193.

21. Hutchinson, "Principles of the Christian Religion," 2:189, 245.

22. Hutchinson, "Principles of the Christian Religion," 2:193.

23. Norbrook, introduction to "Selections from the Theological
Notebook," 2:5.

24. Norbrook, introduction to "Selections from the Theological Notebook," 2:14.

25. Hutchinson, "Principles of the Christian Religion," 2:192.

26. Hutchinson, "Principles of the Christian Religion," 2:237.

27. Hutchinson, "Principles of the Christian Religion," 2:238.

28. When Hutchinson said believers must love God "only," "alone," and
"sole[y]," she meant entirely, uniquely, or "chief[ly]," so as to "loath
. . . all things else in comparison of him." In other words, believers

must love God more than anything else but not to the exclusion of all. Thus, she also wrote that believers must "deny ourselves in all our . . . relations whenever they come in competition with the interest of Christ." Similarly, she exposited Luke 14:26 to say "father and mother are not to be absolutely hated for that elsewhere will appear a great sin but comparatively when they come into competition with Christ." Hutchinson, "Principles of the Christian Religion," 2:257. To say it another way, believers love others "in the Lord as [one's] fellow creature, not . . . [an] idol." Hutchinson, *Memoirs*, 12.

29. Hutchinson, "Principles of the Christian Religion," 2:263.

30. Mark Burden, "Lucy Hutchinson and Puritan Education," *Seventeenth Century* 30 (2015): 167.

31. Lucy Hutchinson, "A briefer summe of what I belieue," in *Works of Lucy Hutchinson*, 2:131. In *Principles of the Christian Religion* Hutchinson clarified that though some churches are less erroneous than others and false churches do exist, Christians should not become so committed to one denomination in a way that effectively excludes all other denominations full of true believers from the universal church. Hutchinson, "Principles of the Christian Religion," 2:119.

32. Lucy Hutchinson, "A briefer summe of what I belieue," 2:119–20.

33. Hutchinson, "A briefer summe of what I belieue," 2:119.

34. Hutchinson, "Principles of the Christian Religion," 2:243.

35. Hutchinson, "Principles of the Christian Religion," 2:271–72.

36. Hutchinson, "Principles of the Christian Religion," 2:272.

37. Hutchinson, "Principles of the Christian Religion," 2:273.

38. Clarke, introduction to "Principles of the Christian Religion," 2:158.

39. *Oxford Dictionary of National Biography*, s.v. "Hutchinson [*née* Apsley], Lucy" by Norbrook.

Chapter 3: Mary Rich

1. Unlike in Lucy Hutchinson's story, Mary's father did not hire a tutor for her and her sisters and thus they did not receive a robust education but rather seemed to focus on skills considered appropriate to women at the time, such as needlework. Sara Heller Mendelson, *The Mental World of Stuart Women: Three Studies* (Brighton, UK: Harvester, 1987), 65, 66.

2. Mary Rich, *Autobiography of Mary Countess of Warwick*, ed. T. Crofton Croker (London: Percy Society, 1748), 3.

3. Eales explains, "Amongst the propertied classes the arrangement of a marriage was regarded primarily as a legal and economic undertaking

and the final choice of a marriage partner was usually the prerogative of the parents. Before the marriage ceremony could take place there would be an exchange of contracts between the fathers of the couple, or their representatives. This provided for the payment of a marriage (more commonly known as the dowry today), and arranged an income known as the 'jointure' for the bride should she be widowed. Matches were made with an eye to the financial advantage provided by a fair dowry and to the social benefits of allying with a wealthy and influential family. It was widely accepted by the early seventeenth century, however, that children should not be forced to marry against their will. Marriage purely for money or for status was increasingly frowned upon and many writers urged that there should be mutual sympathy between bride and groom." Jacqueline Eales, *Puritans and Roundheads* (Glasgow: Hardinge Simpole Publishing, 2002), 19. However, Mary may have still been seen as rebellious in her desires for love and romance as "women may have earned the right to a matrimonial veto by the end of the seventeenth century, but writers continued to insist that modesty forbade women from making their own choice" and romantic love was not seen as a solid foundation for marriage at this time. Mendelson, *Mental World of Stuart Women*, 77.

4. Mendelson, *Mental World*, 80.
5. Rich, *Autobiography*, 7.
6. Rich, *Autobiography*, 8.
7. Rich, *Autobiography*, 27.
8. Rich, *Autobiography*, 21.
9. Mendelson, *Mental World of Stuart Women*, 80.
10. Jennifer O. Venn, "The Autobiographies of 'Barbara Blaugdone, Elizabeth White, Mary Rich, and Mary Penington'" (PhD diss., University of Western Ontario, 1998), 138; Raymond A. Anselment, "Anthony Walker, Mary Rich, and Seventeenth-Century Funeral Sermons of Women," *Prose Studies* 37 (2015): 215.
11. Mendelson, *Mental World of Stuart Women*, 85, 96.
12. Sarah H. Mendelson, "Women and Work," in *A Companion to Early Modern Women's Writing*, ed. Anita Pacheco (Oxford: Blackwell, 2002), 59.
13. Mendelson, *Mental World of Stuart Women*, 100; Mary Rich and Raymond A. Anselment, *The Occasional Meditations of Mary Rich, Countess of Warwick* (Tempe, AZ: Arizona Center for Medieval and Renaissance Studies, 2009), 13.

14. Rich, *Autobiography*, 30.
15. Rich and Anselment, *Occasional Meditations of Mary Rich*, 134, 156. Used by permission.
16. Rich, *Autobiography*, 33–34.
17. Rich, *Autobiography*, 5.
18. Rich, *Autobiography*, 34.
19. Rich, *Autobiography*, 33–34.
20. Raymond A. Anselment, "The Conversion of Mary Rich, Countess of Warwick," *Christianity and Literature* 66 (2017): 602.
21. Mendelson, *Mental World of Stuart Women*, 93.
22. *Oxford Dictionary of National Biography*, s.v. "Rich [*née* Boyle], Mary, countess of Warwick (1624–1678), noblewoman," by Sara H. Mendelson, published in print and online Sep. 23, 2004, https://www.oxforddnb.com.
23. Charlotte Fell Smith, *Mary Rich Countess of Warwick (1625–1678): Her Family & Friends* (London: Longmans, Green, and Co., 1901), 292.
24. Anthony Walker, *Eureka! Eureka! The Virtuous Woman Found* (London: Nathaniel Ranew, 1678), 139.
25. Mary Rich, *Memoir of Lady Warwick: Also Her Diary* (London: The Religious Tract Society, 1799), 128.
26. Rich and Anselment, *Occasional Meditations of Mary Rich*, 134.
27. Rich and Anselment, *Occasional Meditations of Mary Rich*, 66; Rich, *Memoir of Lady Warwick*, 116, 121, 168, 216.
28. Fell Smith, *Mary Rich*, 275.
29. Rich, *Memoir of Lady Warwick*, 164.
30. Rich and Anselment, *Occasional Meditations of Mary Rich*, 77.
31. Joseph Hall, *The Works of Joseph Hall* (Oxford: D. A. Talboys, 1837), 48.
32. Walker, *Eureka!*, 135–36.
33. Walker, *Eureka!*, 136–37.
34. Walker, *Eureka!*, 137–39.
35. Rich and Anselment, *Occasional Meditations of Mary Rich*, 3.
36. Rich and Anselment, *Occasional Meditations of Mary Rich*, 1; Raymond A. Anselment, "Feminine Self-Reflection and the Seventeenth-Century Occasional Meditation," *The Seventeenth Century* 26 (2011): 91n14.
37. Walker, *Eureka!*, 61–62.
38. Rich, *Memoir of Lady Warwick*, 136.
39. Rich and Anselment, *Occasional Meditations of Mary Rich*, 164.

40. Rich and Anselment, *Occasional Meditations of Mary Rich*, 164.

41. Rich and Anselment, *Occasional Meditations of Mary Rich*, 164.

42. Walker, *Eureka!*, 189.

43. Walker, *Eureka!*, 189–90.

44. Walker, *Eureka!*, 190.

45. Rich, *Memoir of Lady Warwick*, 154.

46. Rich and Anselment, *Occasional Meditations of Mary Rich*, 144; Fell Smith, *Mary Rich*, 320; Rich, *Memoir of Lady Warwick*, 72–73.

47. Rich and Anselment, *Occasional Meditations of Mary Rich*, 87.

48. Rich and Anselment, *Occasional Meditations of Mary Rich*, 87.

49. Rich and Anselment, *Occasional Meditations of Mary Rich*, 88.

50. Rich and Anselment, *Occasional Meditations of Mary Rich*, 88.

51. Rich and Anselment, *Occasional Meditations of Mary Rich*, 175.

52. Raymond A. Anselment, "Mary Rich, Countess of Warwick, and the Gift of Tears," *The Seventeenth Century* 22 (2007): 337. Katherine was the wife of Charles II, who served as the king of England during the Restoration.

53. Rich and Anselment, *Occasional Meditations of Mary Rich*, 175–76.

54. Rich and Anselment, *Occasional Meditations of Mary Rich*, 171.

55. Mendelson, "Women and Work," 70.

56. Rich and Anselment, *Occasional Meditations of Mary Rich*, 172.

57. Rich and Anselment, *Occasional Meditations of Mary Rich*, 172.

58. Rich and Anselment, *Occasional Meditations of Mary Rich*, 172.

59. Rich and Anselment, *Occasional Meditations of Mary Rich*, 172.

60. Walker, *Eureka!*, 102.

Chapter 4: Anne Bradstreet

1. Alexander Young, *Chronicles of the First Planters of the Colony of Massachusetts Bay* (Boston: Charles C. Little and James Brown, 1846), 311.

2. Jones Augustine, *The Life and Work of Thomas Dudley, the Second Governor of Massachusetts* (Boston: Hougton, Miflin and Co., 1899), 449.

3. Anne Bradstreet, *The Works of Anne Bradstreet*, ed. Jeannine Hensley (Cambridge: Harvard University Press, 2005), 241. Used by permission.

4. Bradstreet, *Works*, 243.

5. Bradstreet, *Works*, 243.

6. D. B. Kellogg, *Anne Bradstreet* (Nashville, TN: Thomas Nelson, 2010), 144.

7. Bradstreet, *Works*, 178.

8. Margaret Olofson Thickstun, "Contextualizing Anne Bradstreet's Literary Remains: Why We Need a New Edition of the Poems," *Early American Literature* 52 (2017): 409–10.

9. Bradstreet, *Works*, 292.

10. Bradstreet, *Works*, 292.

11. Bradstreet, *Works*, 292.

12. Patricia Phillipy, "Anne Bradstreet's Family Plots: Puritanism, Humanism, Posthumanism," *Criticism* 62 (2020), 51.

13. Bradstreet, *Works*, 292–93.

14. Joshua Bartlett, "Anne Bradstreet's Ecological Thought," *Women's Studies* 43 (2014): 298–99.

15. Bradstreet, *Works*, 232.

16. Bradstreet, *Works*, 202.

17. Bradstreet, *Works*, 288.

18. Bradstreet, *Works*, 293.

19. Allison Giffen, "'Let no man know': Negotiating the Gendered Discourse of Affliction in Anne Bradstreet's 'Here Follows Some Verses Upon the Burning of Our House, July 10th, 1666,'" *Legacy* 27 (2010): 11.

20. Stephanie Pietros, "Anne Bradstreet's 'dear remains': Children and the Creation of Poetic Legacy," *Early Modern Women* (2015): 49.

21. Jacqueline Eales, *Puritans and Roundheads* (Glasgow: Hardinge Simpole Publishing, 2002), 19.

22. Sara Heller Mendelson, *The Mental World of Stuart Women: Three Studies* (Brighton, UK: Harvester, 1987), 188.

23. Bradstreet, *Works*, 235.

24. Bradstreet, *Works*, 258.

25. Bradstreet, *Works*, 235. Here, "blown" means "blossomed."

26. Bradstreet, *Works*, 236.

27. Bradstreet, *Works*, 236.

28. Bradstreet, *Works*, 273–74.

29. Bradstreet, *Works*, 273–74.

30. Bradstreet, *Works*, 237.

31. Bradstreet, *Works*, 237.

32. Bradstreet, *Works*, 237.

33. Bradstreet, *Works*, 237.

34. Bradstreet, *Works*, 237.

35. Bradstreet, *Works*, 238.

36. Bradstreet, *Works*, 204.

37. Bradstreet, *Works*, 234.
38. Bradstreet, *Works*, 238.
39. Bradstreet, *Works*, 238.
40. Bradstreet, *Works*, 238.
41. Bradstreet, *Works*, 238–39.
42. Bradstreet, *Works*, 239.
43. Kellogg, *Anne Bradstreet*, 147; Heidi L. Nichols, *Anne Bradstreet: A Guided Tour of the Life and Thought of a Puritan Poet* (Phillipsburg: P&R Publishing, 2006), 149.
44. Bradstreet, *Works*, 255.
45. Sarah H. Mendelson, "Women and Work," in *A Companion to Early Modern Women's Writing*, ed. Anita Pacheco (Oxford: Blackwell, 2002), 58.
46. Bradstreet, *Works*, 243.

Chapter 5: Brilliana Harley

1. Johanna Harris, "'Scruples and Ceremonies': Lady Brilliana Harley's Epistolary Combat," *Parergon* 29 (2012): 93. In the seventeenth century, the royalists were those who supported King Charles I (in opposition to the parliamentarians).
2. Joanne H. Wright, "Not Just Dutiful Wives and Besotted Ladies: Epistemic Agency in War Writing of Brilliana Harley and Margaret Cavendish," *Early Modern Women* 4 (2009): 9.
3. Jacqueline Eales, *Puritans and Roundheads* (Glasgow: Hardinge Simpole Publishing, 2002), 168, 173.
4. *Oxford Dictionary of National Biography*, "Harley [*née* Conway], Brilliana, Lady Harley (bap. 1598, d. 1643), parliamentarian gentlewoman," by Jacqueline Eales, published in print and online Sept. 23, 2004, https://www.oxforddnb.com; Eales, *Puritans and Roundheads*, 22.
5. Raymond A. Anselment, "Katherine Paston and Brilliana Harley: Maternal Letters and the Genre of Mother's Advice," *Studies in Philology* 101 (2004): 435.
6. Johanna Harris, "Lady Brilliana Harley's Letters and Puritan Intellectual Culture," *Literature Compass* 93 (2012): 263.
7. Diana G. Barnes, "Wifely 'Affection and Disposition': Brilliana Harley and Thomas Gataker's A Wife in Deed (1623)," *English Studies* 98 (2017): 724
8. Barnes, "Wifely 'Affection and Disposition,'" 724.
9. Eales, *Puritans and Roundheads*, 172.

10. Barnes, "Wifely 'Affection and Disposition,'" 724; *Oxford Dictionary of National Biography*, "Harley [*née* Conway], Brilliana," by Eales.

11. *Oxford Dictionary of National Biography*, "Harley [*née* Conway], Brilliana," by Eales.

12. Anselment, "Katherine Paston and Brilliana Harley," 450; Elizabeth Anne Gross, "Domestic Agents: Women, War and Literature in Early Modern England" (PhD diss., Pennsylvania State University, 2006), 244.

13. Eales, *Puritans and Roundheads*, 170.

14. Eales, *Puritans and Roundheads*, 170, 174.

15. Brilliana Harley, *Letters of the Lady Brilliana Harley, Wife of Sir Robert Harley, of Brampton Bryan, Knight of the Bath. With Introd. and Notes by Thomas Taylor Lewis* (London: Camden Society, 1854), 15.

16. Harley, *Letters*, 28, 24, 65, 80.

17. Harley, *Letters*, 10, 15, 12.

18. Harley, *Letters*, 20, 92.

19. Harley, *Letters*, 20, 15.

20. Harley, *Letters*, 7.

21. Harley, *Letters*, 16.

22. Harley, *Letters*, 71.

23. Harley, *Letters*, 69, 20, 42.

24. Harley, *Letters*, 69–70. Numbers added.

25. Harley, *Letters*, 70.

26. Harley, *Letters*, 34.

27. Harley, *Letters*, 20.

28. Harley, *Letters*, 16.

29. Harley, *Letters*, 81.

30. Eales, *Puritans and Roundheads*, 25; Gross, "Domestic Agents," 227; Harley, *Letters*, 44.

31. Harley, *Letters*, 21.

32. Harley, *Letters*, 54. Eales explains that "for many parents the choice of a tutor was more important than the choice of a college. . . . The tutor was expected to act" as a guardian in place of the parent. Eales, *Puritans and Roundheads*, 26.

33. Harley, *Letters*, 55.

34. Harley, *Letters*, 59.

35. Harley, *Letters*, 186, 187.

36. Johanna Harris, "Gestural Dignity: Early Modern Intergenerational Letters of Advice," *Literature and Medicine* 38 (2020): 337, 340.

37. Harley, *Letters*, 166.
38. Harley, *Letters*, 150.
39. Harley, *Letters*, 127.
40. Harley, *Letters*, 78; Eales, *Puritans and Roundheads*, 118.
41. Harley, *Letters*, 84.
42. Sara Read, *Menstruation and the Female Body in Early Modern England* (London: Palgrave Macmillan, 2013), 29, 91.
43. Harley, *Letters*, 16.
44. Harley, *Letters*, 209.
45. Harley, *Letters*, 11.
46. Harley, *Letters*, 61.
47. Harley, *Letters*, 9.
48. Eales, *Puritans and Roundheads*, 24.
49. Harley, *Letters*, 36.
50. Harley, *Letters*, 46.
51. Harley, *Letters*, 47.
52. Harley, *Letters*, 20.
53. Harley, *Letters*, 39.
54. Harley, *Letters*, 204.
55. Harley, *Letters*, 76.
56. Harley, *Letters*, 119–20.
57. Eales, *Puritans and Roundheads*, 170, 174.
58. Richard Baxter, *Reliquiae Baxterianae*, ed. Matthew Sylvester (London: T. Parkhurst, J. Robinson, J. Lawrence, and J. Dunton, 1696), 59–60.
59. *Oxford Dictionary of National Biography*, "Harley, Sir Edward (1624–1700), politician and parliamentarian army officer," by Gordon Goodwin and David Whitehead, published in print and online Sept. 23, 2004, https://www.oxforddnb.com.
60. Harley, *Letters*, 248.
61. Eales, *Puritans and Roundheads*, 195.

General Index